THE SPIRIT OF
BRITISH ADMINISTRATION
and some European comparisons

C. H. SISSON

with a foreword by
PROFESSOR W. J. M. MACKENZIE

FABER AND FABER LTD
24 Russell Square
London

First published in mcmlix
by Faber and Faber Limited
24 Russell Square London W.C.1
Second edition mcmlxvi
Printed in Great Britain by
Latimer Trend & Co Ltd Whitstable

© *C. H. Sisson*

1959

Preface to the Second Edition

I

The point of view of the working administrator is not one of which much is heard in the general discussion of public administration. The experts are men of another trade—academics who have had more or less contact with the practical business of Whitehall, or lawyers, who have their own axes to grind. The lawyers' axes are very good ones, and the special interests of the academic may give him a clear perception of certain aspects of administration. The administrator, whose mind is formed by the necessity of taking account of other people's points of view and conciliating interests, would not wish to exclude the contributions which can come to the study of administration from either of these sources. But he may feel that he has a valid point of view of his own. No official can claim to express a representative view—officials are, anyway, trained not to make such claims—and it must be admitted that one who expresses himself in public about such matters does so by an aberration from the habits of his kind.

The legal critic of Whitehall is likely to make much of freedom—and to mean freedom from civil servants but not freedom from lawyers. The academic critic may talk of efficiency and of public access to information about the ways in which public monies are disbursed—but not mean efficiency in universities or a more searching light on the way they spend the taxpayer's money. While there is every reason why the legal and academic lynxes should turn their eyes on Whitehall, if you are interested in its working you might also like to know what the mole thinks as he works underground there. It is a sort of evidence about the system, even if your conclusions are more far-sighted than his.

The limitations of the administrator's view of Whitehall will come, in part at least, from his concern that the system shall be one that *works*. No doubt the conception of what is meant by the system working is a difficult one, and the administrator's view of efficiency will, like everyone else's, be limited. A business man who saw the efficiency of his enterprise too exclusively in terms of the profits of his shareholders might end by being a bit of a nuisance in the economy as well as a benefit. You would not, however, think of pronouncing on the efficiency of a business without paying very serious attention to what the business man had to say about profits. The criteria of efficiency in the public service are certainly no less complex—indeed it can be argued that they are more so, because the range of reference is wider— and the administrator's view of what is needed to make the thing work is not something which experts from other fields, or the public at large, can afford to be too supercilious about. The seasoned administrator, in Whitehall, has a sense of what can be done, of the extent to which what often seem to him the vague ideas of the outside world can be carried into effect, as acute as the entrepreneur's sense of what will make profit for his concern. Like the entrepreneur, the administrator in White- hall can be wrong. Or accidents may occur by the way which result in him being given credit for being right when his judge- ment at the crucial moment was wrong. Or he may be blamed for being wrong when in fact he saw all that could be seen at the time of decision. Practical affairs are very confusing.

It is very difficult, in particular, for anyone who has not sat near the centre of a great government department to have a sense of that situation. On one side of the senior administrator is the political world, more rough and ready, but with its roots in tradition and in public passions and its antennae feeling, more or less fumblingly, into all the corners of our social and econo- mic life. On the other side an administrative machine of a size which has no rival in private enterprise, a machine partly very modern, partly antiquated, to which bits have been added for all kinds of opportunist reasons as well as in answer to more enduring needs. 'On the one side, on the other side'—I am aware that these expressions might seem to betray unconstitu- tional thoughts and to suggest a rebellion—the existence of which is often suspected and is indeed a favourite theme of academic critics—against political direction. It is, however, one

Preface to the Second Edition

of the complexities of the situation that it includes an iron discipline and an unquestioning subordination to political chiefs. I have avoided the expressions 'above' and 'below'—the politicians above and the administrative machine below—because the political considerations involve more than mere subordination to a minister and the administrative considerations more than the machine a particular administrator happens to direct himself. All the considerations the administrator at work has to take account of appear rather as things at his elbow; in a complicated business obedience is no more straightforward than command. A minister would have as little reason to thank an official who thought his function consisted in saying 'Yes, sir' as a subordinate in the service would have reason to be pleased with a superior who took decisions without listening carefully for the worried and confused evidences which come from below. It is a question often mooted how far, in this world of vast bureaucracies, ministerial responsibility is a reality. The question is more easily understood by someone who has worked in a great organization than by someone who has not. Of course the minister does not and cannot take all decisions himself, any more than the subordinate official or the branch manager of an industrial or commercial enterprise can take all the decisions in matters within his field of control. Moreover, the minister takes over, when he comes into office, a complex organization which he can at best modify a little. But within these limits—which are limits imposed by the nature of things and not by the wilful scheming of officials—the minister's authority is absolute. How much it would help him to discharge his responsibilities if the working of the subordinate échelons were perpetually open to public scrutiny is a matter for argument; and the answer no doubt is, sometimes more, sometimes less. An official who resisted such scrutiny might be merely protecting himself and his colleagues from criticism. He might, however, legitimately think that officials ought to be allowed to get on with their work like other people, and that if public business is to be despatched with reasonable speed and at not too exorbitant a cost it is necessary to set some limit to the curiosity of outside critics— who are sometimes rather presumptuous when they attribute to themselves all the dignity of 'the public'. The official may properly be suspect, but he is not necessarily wrong, when he pleads that particular decisions have to be judged in a wide context and that the ordinary operation of a Department, headed by a minister who is a member of the government and answerable to Parliament, is by no means the worst way of doing this. To be sure it is not the only way and there is everything to be said for as much openness as is consistent with efficiency.

The problem of ministerial responsibility is connected with another—the extent to which the official is responsive to parliamentary and public pressures, and the extent to which he takes initiatives and gets his own way. It may be that one or two academics, whose practical experience in Whitehall is limited to a few years, in not very exalted situations, in the peculiar and chaotic conditions of war, underestimate that responsiveness because, at the time and with the subject matters they were concerned with, such responsiveness was not part of the mechanism of their work. But the ordinary administrator, in peace-time, is much concerned with the parliamentary and public position of his minister. Of course this counts for more in some subjects than with others, because the operation of public consciousness is such that it is not equally aware of, or interested in, all aspects of public business at all times. Many administrators would, I think, say that the account of the administrative process given in the first chapter of this book, and assumed throughout, makes so much of this responsiveness that it gives the administrator an unrealistically negative character. My account is over-simplified. In fact the notion of responsiveness is no simpler than the notion of the relationships implied in obedience. The official has a duty—an almost unlimited one—to understand the way things are going, in order to be able to suggest measures appropriate to the times. This will involve him in an active exchange of facts and ideas and a habit of mental exploration. In these matters he certainly should not, and I hope generally does not, show up as more passive or less inventive than his academic or legal critics or than the enterprising director or manager in industry or commerce. It remains true, however, that the inventiveness of the administrator is secondary to the acceptability of his ideas. Great careers have been made, in the civil service as elsewhere, out of a sharp sense of the way the cat will

Preface to the Second Edition

jump. If the man whose career is made that way is not likely to be among those most highly regarded by his colleagues it has to be admitted that a certain talent in cat-watching is an indispensable qualification for the higher reaches. A good idea is no good unless it fits into the context of the time, has a place in the universe of discourse within which, by consensus, the discussion of public affairs is conducted. Of course the administrator, like the academic, or any of the other numerous classes which contribute to the discussion of our affairs, may contribute to that gradual change in the public universe of discourse which goes on all the time. He is, moreover, better placed than most for making his contribution at the most fruitful moment. But the truth is that public affairs are, inevitably, largely conducted in terms of second-hand ideas. An idea widely enough accepted to be the basis for political action is already on the way to being a superstition, in the strict sense. The real inventiveness of the human race is usually to be found not at the centre but at the periphery, and in a democracy it can hardly be otherwise. The consciousness of tomorrow is formed by peculiar people who have no special business at the centre. The artist, by which I mean the artist and not the prize-winner in the art trade, is the typical case.

It follows that a great deal of patience goes to the conduct of government, in which the sort of administrator we are talking about is a technician. A man in this business has to learn not to over-value his own ideas. Enough sense has to be made out of the superstitions and clamours of the time to ensure that the ship of state—a metaphor as precise as one could wish—keeps on its way. The administrator by himself certainly cannot ensure this. He is a part of the directing equipment, no more. It is one of the advantages of studying administration by a comparative method that the importance of history and geography, of traditions and resources, and the *relative* unimportance of administrative procedures and techniques, spring to notice. That is not to say that these things are themselves unimportant. With the growth in the size of bureaucracies, and the continuous widening of the circle of matters in which governments interest themselves, they are of great and increasing importance. The subject-matter of this book is limited to what goes on in government but comparisons of other kinds may also be useful.

ix

Preface to the Second Edition

In particular one would look to industry. It is not that there is a secret of efficiency waiting to be transferred from industry or elsewhere to the government service. Efficiency is not that kind of thing. It is no more than the suitability and economy of means in relation to ends. What it consists in in a particular organization can be fully understood only by someone who knows a good deal about the ends for which the organization exists and the means it is possible to employ in it. But there are certainly some flexibilities in industrial organization which could with advantage be introduced into the government service, though some of the most desirable are, for reasons rooted deep in the nature of the government's situation, very difficult to introduce. There are certainly advantages—reciprocal advantages, there is reason to believe—to be got by comparisons between the organization of industry and government, but although great claims are sometimes made for organizational studies there is probably more to be got by less formal, less academic methods, the mere circulation of notions and people.

II

This book had its origin in an article I wrote some years ago for *The Cambridge Journal*, under the editorship of Professor Michael Oakeshott. A good deal of this article is reproduced in the first chapter, where what two or three civil servants of our own day have said about their trade is set beside the observations of Samuel Pepys on the work of the Navy Office in the seventeenth century and those of Frontinus on the organization of the Roman aqueducts towards the end of the first century A.D. The hope was that this juxtaposition would make it possible to discard what is merely local and temporary in our view of public administration and bring to light some of the more permanent elements. This germinal essay was the result of the confluence of two long-standing interests. On the one hand I had been, since 1936, and with an interruption only for service elsewhere during the war, a member of the Administrative Class of the Home Civil Service—paid therefore to understand administration so far as understanding is necessary for performance in this field. On the other hand I had, for at least as long, been concerned with the problem of government in a more theoretical way, and as a by-product of my reading had contributed articles to several journals and in particular, with some regularity, to *The New English Weekly*, where Mr. Philip Mairet not only permitted me to review current books on government and related subjects but to bring into the reckoning Junius, Vauvenargeues, Choderlos de Laclos—whatever I happened to be reading. So in my essay for *The Cambridge Journal* I was writing not merely as a civil servant who wanted to say something about administration but as a student of government who happened also to be a practising administrator. It was in this dual role that, when I was fortunate enough to be given a research fellowship by Manchester University and a sabbatical year by the Civil Service, I set off to look at the way in which various European countries managed their public services. Obviously I could not make anything like a comprehensive study of so large a subject. But I hoped, after some years of attention to the processes of government, and of experience as a practising administrator, to get a glimpse of the practices of other countries and to set what I saw against what I knew, at first hand, of what went on in Whitehall. The question at the back of my mind as I visited some of my opposite numbers in their offices in Paris, Bonn, Vienna, Stockholm, Madrid and one or two provincial centres was: How does this office work? What would it be like to be in that man's shoes and, if I were, how should I get my work done? This gave my conversations, and the texts I read, an interest of a different kind from that some academic students have found in similar explorations. Professor Hamson (*v.* Chapter IV), in studying the operation of the *Conseil d'état,* was interested in impeding the executive—in the legitimate interests, of course, of presumed individual rights. My interest at the Palais Royal was to discover how the executive managed to live with certain impediments—a less popular but not less real problem. Before I went to Stockholm I had heard, from some of my academic colleagues at Manchester, almost ecstatic praises of the Swedish law (p. 105) which requires that official documents should be open to the public; I was told that we ought to follow the Swedish example and open all the files of Whitehall to the inspection of dons and journalists. I could see some inconveniences in this, and did not believe that the Swedes or anyone else really ran their government machine in this way (would any business dream of conducting its affairs in this manner?). So my interest in Stockholm was to find out how government departments in fact operated against a legal background of this character. Swedish officials had, as I expected, found a way. And so with my enquiries about centralization and decentralization in Germany, France and elsewhere. Someone has to work these systems and how they are worked has an importance hardly less than that of the constitutional principles they are alleged to embody. My interest in politicians was, likewise, an interest in how the officials lived with them and succeeded in carrying out the directions of their chiefs. If this is a less important subject than some other questions which can be asked about politicians—the habitual democratic discussion about the policies they stand for—it is a question which has very great importance none the less. For although in the nature of the case it is less easy for an outsider than for an insider to understand how a civil service works, it is certainly of importance to everybody that it should work, in the ordinary executive sense in which an industrial or commercial organization has to work.

The six years which have passed since the publication of this book have changed certain emphases, in the world of public administration as well as in my own view of it, but they have not changed the principles here elicited and brought into play. The political changes in France have made little difference in the general lines of the administration; and such changes as there have been in the prefectoral system have certainly not been out of line with the principles established by the First Consul. At home there has been some elaboration of the training of the young administrator and a Centre for Administrative Studies has been set up. But this eighteen weeks' tuition, taken in the course of ordinary probation in a Department and unaccompanied by any change in the method of recruitment, has certainly not changed the character of the service nor was it meant to do so. We are promised an Ombudsman, so that one academic dream at least has come true, but the innovation is being made with due regard to our Parliamentary system and the practice of ministerial responsibility, so that it is a technical rather than a constitutional change.

Preface to the Second Edition

III

Perhaps, finally, I may try to disarm one or two misunderstandings to which the book was subject on its first appearance. Because it attempts to describe what is, rather than what ought to be, the outlook and ethos of the British administration, it was sometimes held to be a tract directed against all innovation. This is rubbish. But as one would be foolish to innovate in the Courts without trying first to understand what lawyers are at, or in universities without an acute sense of what goes on there, so the only realistic basis for the reform of the Civil Service is an understanding of its constitutional situation and habitual attitudes, simply because they are the facts of the case. There is no reason why the official should dislike change; indeed life is a great deal more interesting for him when he is at a centre of change than when he is not. I am, as it happens, deeply attached to that vague entity, the British Constitution. But I have certainly no desire to preserve the Civil Service as it is, still less to preserve a particular Civil Service class—which is after all little more than a nomenclature. If I am disinclined to see lay administrators replaced by experts it is simply because I do not know where to look for the experts who would do precisely the job which administrators in Whitehall have to do. The truth is that, not merely in our system, but in any system of humane government, the ultimate decisions cannot be taken within the limits of any academic discipline. They are taken within the discipline of practical affairs; their justification is their success. But if that is not to become the most destructive of will-o'-the-wisps, somewhere, and however dimly, the end of government has to be glimpsed. By this I do not mean that we want governors— certainly not civil servants—who think they can define the end of government and will govern in accordance with their definition. The end is something which should not so much be written into the constitution as built into it, so that it is implicit in the milieu in which we work. It is in this respect that, I venture to think, history has left us more fortunate than the other countries at which, in this book, I have taken a sidelong glance.

September, 1965   C.H.S.

Contents

1

Contents

Contents

Plus je lis ce qu'ils appellent les principes du *Droit public*, plus je me convaincs de l'inanité des règles et des généralités sur cette matière.

Barbey d'Aurevilly

Foreword

In England we all criticize the Civil Service. For most of us, this is like talk about the weather; a good way to open conversation because you can be pretty certain that the other man will also have something to say on the subject. For some, perhaps, there is a half-conscious touch of self-assertion. To link together two quotations from *Pinafore*:

> 'His energetic fist should be ready to resist
> A dictatorial word . . .'
> 'He is an Englishman—behold him!'

And there are a few for whom this is a sort of politics. Dr. Johnson in his parliamentary reporting took care 'that the *Whig Dogs* should not have the best of it'. Some critics of administration take care that the Socialist dogs should not have a leg left to stand on. For them the Coal Board becomes emotionally involved with Crichel Down, rockets in the Hebrides with Liverpool's water supply from Wales, bummarees at Smithfield with cups of tea in the office; and the whole savoury lump is salted with personalities.

But the topic also has its intellectuals. Much has been written by lawyers, political scientists and publicists in the attempt to set out, quietly, seriously and coherently, what is wrong with British administration and what should be done to put it right. But there is (after all) in logic another possibility: perhaps our odd arrangements are (this being an imperfect world) as good as any others open to us, within the limits of our situation; perhaps the working of British administration is as native to us as our habit of criticizing it, perhaps we and our administration exist together as constituents of an indivisible political system.

Foreword

This is Mr. Sisson's main theme, but it leads him into many questions of constitutional theory and comparative politics. Criticism in the academic style almost always involves two elements; a view of the British constitution, as it is and as it should be, including a view of the place in it of the Civil Service; a comparison of the institutions of central administration in Britain with those of other large organizations, public and private. One can take one's choice of constitutional principles, according to temperament and according to what one wants to prove. Some critics emphasize that government is by law established, and that law is the condition of freedom; others, that government is in the last resort an act of will, that legitimate government expresses the will of a free people, and that the people must through its government have power to act. One can take either line (even —at a pinch—both lines together); but in either event it is natural to mix abstract argument with examples drawn from other countries and other organizations (the analogy with large private corporations is now important) which are believed to do things better than we do them.

There are two main schools of criticism. First, there are those who think most of control, asking that the Civil Service should be better trained in law and more effectively controlled by courts of law—like the French Civil Service in relation to the *Conseil d'Etat*; that the internal procedure of the Service should be standardized by publicly known regulations—as in the countries of the old Hapsburg sphere of influence; that this internal procedure should be open to public view and criticism, so that the names of individual civil servants are associated with particular acts and decisions—as happens in Sweden. Secondly, there are those who allege that the Civil Service is inefficient as an instrument of government; that the 'class' system of entry makes it socially conservative and less 'democratic' than the Civil Services of those countries (primarily the Australasian dominions) which have no separate Administrative Class; that it has no means of absorbing and training scientists and technologists for the highest levels of administration—as has France; that its horizon is restricted by the daily cycle of travel between a London suburb and a London office, and that there will be no 'red blood' in the Administrative Class until it gets out into the field

6

Foreword

and does a 'real job'—like the prefects in France and Spain, or the District Commissioners in our own Overseas Service; that it has no notion of 'scientific management' and the other techniques of big business organization, as worked out by private industry and its satellite consultants and professors, especially in the U.S.A.; finally (and above all), that it is a clog on effective government because it is unresponsive to public sentiment and the changing of the political guard—higher civil servants are not in this country known for their party affiliations, as in France and in the U.S.A.

This long (but incomplete) list indicates the existence of an academic field about which politicians, civil servants and the public on the whole know little and care less. Mr. Sisson perhaps knows it as (on his view) a good civil servant knows the subject-matter of the business he has to transact; not exhaustively, but enough for the purposes of the argument—and his argument is a somewhat subtle one. The defender cannot of course deny that these contrasts exist; they can be documented quite readily, and personal acquaintance soon gives an idea of what they mean in practice. The line of defence (and counter-attack) is that these contrasts define but do not discredit British administration. By defining it, they give clues as to the way in which its characteristics are interrelated, and how they are together part of a particular 'climate' (in the sense of Montesquieu), a political context which gives each of them a meaning not the same as its meaning in isolation.

Montesquieu himself has posthumously experienced some of the risks of this way of proceeding. It is easier to express such ideas by illustration than by formal theory. Montesquieu's own theories (if one looks at them in the original) are rather delicately elusive; pinned down and made consistent by patient students, they become positively false. Mr. Sisson's theory therefore is not easy to handle. Perhaps its essence lies in seeking to adopt, as the creed of the Civil Service, a particular view of the nature of government. M. Mendès-France is quoted as saying that 'to govern is to choose'. For Mr. Sisson to govern is primarily to adjust; to maintain unity in a society by avoiding choices which must in their nature be divisive, in the end cumulatively destructive. *Primarily* to adjust; not wholly, because there are occasions when in the last resort a choice must be made and imposed. But in our constitutional system there is a specialization of function. It is for the politician to choose, for the permanent servants of the Crown (a category wider than that of civil servant) to adjust.

Criticisms at once come to mind; as one reads one finds that most of them have come to Mr. Sisson's mind also. Is there a touch of Podsnappery, of imperviousness, about this way of talking about other countries? 'They do, Sir, they do—I am sorry to be obliged to say it—*as* they do.' Perhaps; but it is an important fact about the British civil servant that

> 'he might have been a Roosian,
> A French, or Turk, or Proosian,
> Or perhaps Itali-an'—

but is not.

Does the author speak too exclusively for the Administrative Class, as it works in the civilian sector, in a period of relative peace? Does he neglect the policy-makers in the Foreign Service, the Chiefs of Staff, the scientists, the engineers? Perhaps: but his case is that in the last resort the whole system depends on the House of Commons, and that for all permanent servants of the Crown the ultimate test of success in administration is that they should give their Minister a case which will stand up to criticism by expert debaters, in public. This attitude is of central importance in the 'democratic' control of administration, as we understand democracy. If there are large areas of British administration in which the attitude no longer exists, then Mr. Sisson is wrong: the system has changed radically, its centre (if it still has one) lies elsewhere than in the House of Commons. This would be a much more important change than the formal threats to the formal sovereignty of Parliament about which so much has been written. Has it been an anxious matter in recent years for administrators to brief Ministers, and to act so that they feel they can securely brief Ministers, on such secret matters as Middle Eastern policy, the development of atomic weapons, the re-equipment of the R.A.F.? It is not easy for an outside observer to judge how matters are going; but it looks as if the pressure of the House of Commons is still felt, even by the diplomats, the scientists and the Air Marshals. If this is so, Mr. Sisson's 'model' is not yet obsolete.

Some may feel that in taking this high (though practical) view of the role of the politicians Mr. Sisson depresses too far the importance of the permanent service of the Crown, that he under-rates it, and in doing so evades responsibility. He does indeed inculcate humility, not 'the pride that apes humility', but a genuine humility which is a skill necessary to the performance of a service deserving pride. Readers will not find false modesty in his concluding chapter: rather a pride in the nature of a situation not easily understood except by those who share it. Civil servants, after all, are (as he says) men who 'might, in the last desperation, exhibit a scruple'. This is their pride, and their humility.

Manchester University,   W. J. M. MACKENZIE
September 1958

Author's Note

This is an attempt at a character study of the permanent administration in Whitehall, drawn against a background which, to my mind, shows up clearly what the essential peculiarities of that body are. The background is an account of those features of certain European administrations which contrast most strongly with our own practice. Just as, in a more general way, one may understand better what England is like when one has seen a little of other western countries, or understand better what Europe is like when one has looked at it from Asia, so one's view of what goes on in Whitehall may be sharpened if, after twenty years of practice there, one has found oneself successively in Paris, Bonn, Vienna, Stockholm, and Madrid, to say nothing of one or two provincial centres abroad, in the offices of men who practise the art of administration in those places. That explains, in general terms, the origin and purpose of this book, which was made possible by the tenure of a Simon Senior Research Fellowship in the University of Manchester.

I should like to thank the Senate and Council of the University of Manchester for giving me the opportunity to make this study, and in particular Professor W. J. M. Mackenzie for his unobtrusive and always helpful advice, as well as other members of the staff whose lively expression of their views on civil services here and abroad has been of great value to me in the formulation of my own views. I should also like to thank the numerous officials in the countries I visited for the courtesy and good humour with which they satisfied my no doubt tiresome curiosity.

C.H.S.

CHAPTER I

What Administration Is

When a Minister announces in the House that he will *do* something he is rarely talking about the sort of thing that he himself *does*. What he does, as Minister, is to attend cabinet meetings, make speeches, explain to deputations how the government regards certain matters that affect them, discuss with his senior officials how his Department's business should be conducted, and sign or—not less important—refuse to sign the letters prepared for him. When he tells the House he will do something he is, however, in effect supplying a small or greater impulsion which, transmitted through the system of connections provided by the Civil Service, in the characteristic case results in something being done for or to some member of the public, perhaps by some not very eminent official miles from Westminster. There is a long concatenation, and the people in it are so numerous, their activities so multifarious, the organizations they form are so permanent, as compared with the relative impermanence of what are thought of as elected governments—though governments are not, as such, elected at all—that it is more usual to speak of what a Minister is *responsible for* than of what he does.

Near the centre, that is to say, near the Minister, there is a group of officials, now usually fairly numerous, who, whatever the subject-matter of their particular work, may be said to specialize in the awareness of ministerial responsibility. It is not only they who have this awareness, which is much more widely diffused, and this awareness is not the only concern of the members of the group—though all they do could perhaps be reduced to it. But in the work they have to do, the members of this group are nearer to being a bit of the Minister's mind, nearer to his point of view than are officials who are further from the Minister either geographically or, wherever they may be stationed, in the nature of their concerns.

A group of officials roughly answering to this description is to be found in every ministry in Europe. It would not always be easy to define the group with precision. There are always certain senior people who unquestionably belong to it; the difficulty is only in determining the lower limits of the group. In Great Britain there is supposed to be a special class of the Civil Service corresponding to this function—the Administrative Class. Roughly speaking it does so correspond. To this class Permanent Secretaries, Under Secretaries, Assistant Secretaries and Principals belong and these people have those concerns in their hands. The extent to which an individual member of the class is preoccupied in this manner depends on what happens to be his job at the moment, and on what happens to be, at the moment, the public interest in what he is doing, and there are of course officials outside the Administrative Class who have a share in this sort of concern. One may, however, speak of this concern as being the characteristic preoccupation of the Administrative Class and it is with administration, in the sense in which that word has meaning in relation to the operations of that class of the British Civil Service, that this book is concerned.

What is involved in that job, leaving aside the several subjects with which administrators are concerned? It includes contributing to the advice given to Ministers in relation to the decisions they have to take. This contribution is both direct, as in the production of memoranda to be placed before Ministers and in personal discussion with them, and indirect, by way of the minutes, memoranda and discussions which make up the researches and deliberations which generally precede the giving of advice. The job includes, of course, the preparation of replies to parliamentary questions and to the Minister's correspondence from M.P.s and others, and of briefs for parliamentary debates or for use by the Minister when he receives deputations; it also includes the transaction, on his behalf and within defined terms of reference, of a great deal of business of which the details do not generally come to the Minister but which is consistent with his statutory obligations and is of such a character that it may be supposed to have his general approval. The job includes, also, directing the work of subordinates in the current of the Minister's mind. The 'current of the Minister's mind' is partly an individual current, more or less strong according to the measure of his ability or idiosyncrasy, partly a party current— political in the vulgar sense. Still more it expresses the sense which the government as a whole has of the necessities of its situation, and this sense, in turn, is determined by the nature of the constitutional system.

The Minister is, like Wordsworth's poet, 'a man speaking to men', and just as the remotest discoveries of the chemist or the mineralogist may become material for the poet as soon as they begin to change the feelings and relations of ordinary people, so the Minister is interested in a speciality, whether in the organization of his ministry or in a technical or scientific development outside, as soon as it exhibits something of actual or potential political importance. The Minister does not, unless in his private leisure, promenade for pleasure or instruction in the fields of science or of social studies. What he does, characteristically, is to take a decision. The decision may be one involving physics, or medicine or chemistry, but it involves at the same time a number of other elements as well. Even when the most abstruse matters come to his notice the Minister is not playing at being a scientist or a specialist of any sort. He is adhering to his proper political rôle of taking notice of things which have become of public concern. And he has to take notice of them in the context provided by the law of the land and the policy of the government of which he is a member.

The question of how much a Minister should bring himself to understand of a speciality with which he has to deal is not one that can be answered in general terms. How much he does may depend on the importance, in political terms, of the problem to be settled, as well as on his previous training and the measure of his curiosity. There may be cases in which, although the problem is at first sight a scientific one, the only practical issue to be decided is which of two warring factions within a speciality could more safely be followed, and for such a problem the deciding point is the respective standing of the factions within the relevant professional field and, if the great public as well as various little publics are involved, the acceptability of the professional authority to the electorate at large. The problem of finding acceptable authorities is, however, rarely entirely separable from a judgment on matters on the fringe of the specialist field. For the Minister who has to take a political decision, the specialist is merely an adviser, and the conscious and responsible taker of advice does not accept it without understanding it. He may be urged to take measures which, on examination, prove to have, besides the main results which the specialist hopes to achieve by them, consequences which would render them odious in the extreme. The standard of odium is not a matter on which the expert is expert. The Minister has to make sure that he is in possession of all the information that he needs about the results and risks of the course of action he is advised to take, whether or not they are relevant to the objective the specialist has in mind, and he has to place that information in a context which is not less wide than the political complex of aims and pressure in which the cabinet acts. It is because the decision to be taken is so much wider than the speciality that senior administrative officials have to learn to extract from the specialist flowers around them the honey their Minister needs, explaining as they do so that the Minister does not live on honey.

The Minister has to defend his decision in Parliament, and the central place of parliamentary apologetics in our administrative system, and the fact that, however unplausible that may seem, they are a principle of coherence and order in it, can hardly be overstressed. At the administrative centre of a government department the concerns of the physicist, the medical man or the engineer have to be looked at in the context of what the government intends and what Ministers can reasonably say to the House. Although this is sometimes a matter of resentment it means no more than that this country retains enough of the fruits of the Reformation to prefer to be governed in a language that is 'understanded of the people'. Just as it is in general the popularizers of ideas, not the rare brains who invent, who are of immediate practical political concern, so it is ultimately not the science, but the consequences of it which are popularly appreciable and politically relevant, that are matters of concern to Ministers. The assumption of our system of government is that, at this point, minor or particular pressures will disappear or at least fall into place in the national scheme of pressures. There is, of course, no magic about the House of Commons as an index of forces, and any particular critic may make a good show of demonstrating that, in some matter dear to him, the House's index was in some way unsatisfactory. The point about the index is, however, not whether it is a true index, as measured by some outside standard, but that it is constitutionally and in fact the standard by which the acts and proposals of government are tested. It is no doubt open to the critic of government machinery to say, if he chooses, that the test is a poor one. Everything is open to him. But everything is not open to the Civil Servant. The coherence of the government machinery depends on his acceptance of the constitutional context in which he operates. And the views of this or that critic as to the validity of the test are of negligible practical importance beside the fact that the test does not noticeably discontent the population at large. And even that fact is, from a strictly professional point of view, unimportant to the Civil Servant beside the fact that the test of parliamentary tolerance is the test in fact. The silences of Parliament—for example, its virtual silence on questions of religious politics—are as definitory for the Civil Servant as the most conclusive debates.

Various attempts have been made to reduce to an essential principle the multifarious operations which the British administrator performs in this constitutional context. We are most likely to be brought close by some such personal account as that given by Bridges several years ago. There we read of work which provides, 'and provided to a considerable degree, an intense satisfaction and delight in the accomplishment of difficult tasks, a delight which has much in common with that felt by scholars or even on occasions by artists on the completion of some outstandingly difficult work'.[1] We find also an emphasis on the 'strong corporate life' of the Civil Servant. We find him portrayed as the exponent of a departmental philosophy, 'the resultant of protests and suggestions, and counter suggestions, from many interests', which represents 'an acceptable middle

[1] Sir Edward (now Lord) Bridges, *Portrait of a Profession* (1950), p. 32.

point of view after the extreme divergencies have been rooted out'.[1] Thus we are told two things by Bridges. One is about the affective character of the Civil Servant's work. A man may take pleasure in it because it is difficult. It is not altogether clear why the pleasure, or the difficulty, should be compared with that encountered by the artist or the scholar, who are certainly not the only other people to be confronted with difficult tasks, or to take pleasure in overcoming them, while the corporate character of the Civil Servant's work does not give him any obvious affinity with the artist of modern times, though it might, perhaps, give him a little with the scholar. The second thing we are told is about the opinions the Civil Servant is likely to hold and to contribute as occasion arises to the solution of his Minister's problems. These opinions are not his own. They are a mediocrity arrived at not because they are likely to be true, though sometimes they may even be that, but because in a system of protests and objections a man may hold them and escape without too many rotten eggs plastering his head. Neither of these two points made by Bridges describes the nature of the intellectual operation, if there is one, that the servant of state performs. One must in passing note in Bridges, as in other only less eminent authorities, a conviction, natural enough in those who have spent a lifetime in the Service and have emerged a long way up, that the Service has not only changed beyond all recognition in recent times but has improved to an almost equal degree. Miss Cohen[2] is struck by the improved industry and integrity of the Civil Servant in the last hundred and fifty years. Bridges sees an abatement of departmentalism.[3] C. K. Munro[4] sees men less intent on giving orders and more anxious to serve. None of these observations, not even the last, is entirely without foundation. But none of these improvements, most probably, has been without compensating drawbacks. All of them appear to have been in something subsidiary to the operation of administration. The fact that the improvements are supposed to have been so great suggests that

---

[1] Bridges, p. 17.
[2] Emmeline W. Cohen, *The Growth of the British Civil Service* (1941), passim.
[3] Bridges, pp. 22–23.
[4] C. K. Munro, *The Fountains in Trafalgar Square* (1952), pp. 22–25 et passim.

What Administration Is

they cannot have been in anything permanently essential to the conduct of government. For government has been going on for a long time, and if so much improvement has taken place in its essential procedures we should not have to go far back in history before we came upon a complete anarchy. And looking the other way, we should be uncomfortably near the millennium.

We may take comfort, however. In fact, if we look back three hundred years, we see Samuel Pepys transacting the King's business as aptly as it has generally been done in this century. When we read him our contemporary peculiarities, such as the size of our bureaucracies and the quality of our honesty, are seen as such and we catch a glimpse of whatever it is that enables governments to persist at all. The constitutional changes since 1660 have not been of such a nature as even much to alter certain relations of Parliament and the executive. The modern Civil Servant will recognize himself in this: 'This month ends with my mind full of business and concernment how this office will speed with the Parliament, which begins to be mighty severe in the examining our accounts, and the expense of the Navy this war.'[1] He will recognize the tactician's satisfaction at the diversion caused by the Great Fire: 'He says he hath computed that the rents of houses lost by this fire in the City come to £600,000 per annum; that this will make the Parliament more quiet than otherwise they would have been.'[2] And he will know the feelings, which are in the very marrow of the profession, described in the words: 'Reckoning myself to come off with victory, because not overcome in anything or much foiled.'[3]

It has no doubt often been remarked that Frontinus exhibits all the characteristics of the good Civil Servant. It was his task and pleasure, about the year A.D. 97, to reform the administration of the water supply borne into Rome on the great aqueducts. The task had just those characteristics which caused Bridges to reflect that he was almost an artist; but the reflections of Frontinus were different. There were disparities between the records and the facts which no one had bothered to check; there were false measurements which made it impossible for

[1] Samuel Pepys, *Diary*, 30th September 1666.
[2] Pepys, 15th September 1666.   [3] Pepys, 3rd October 1666.

19

the authorities to balance their books. In these matters Frontinus set order, and he pauses in his record only to notice the
superiority of these works of utility over works of mere beauty
such as the Greeks were proud of. *Otiosa sed fama celebrata opera
Graecorum.* Frontinus recognized that his modest function was
to serve in matters that could be commonly appreciated. He was
the man from the water company. But he was not particularly
modest about the manner of his performance. He speaks of 'my
natural sense of responsibility' and 'my fidelity', and pom-
pously insists: 'Those who sought the Emperor's pardon, after
warning received, may thank me for the favour granted.'[1] His
was a typically useful and uninteresting mind.

What are the qualities of mind most needed in the public
servant? As his subject-matter must always be a good that is
not only common but is commonly recognized, he had better
not be in the habit of seeing things with his own eyes, unless
he has an abnormal disinterestedness which enables him at once
to set aside his own vision. Perhaps it is to be preferred that
reality should appear to him exclusively in that form which is
capable of preservation in a number, a name, a date, verbal
forms which are references and not presentations. His concern,
like any philosopher's, is with relationships, but he must always
avoid all those questions of value to which a philosophic study
of relationships is apt to lead. He should have a mind tenacious
of his limited sort of fact, and exclusive of other sorts, and such
a delight in the play of relationships that the question of value
never troubles him. Since great disinterestedness is not always
to be found in combination with the primarily required ability
to perform juggleries with the rigorously limited fact, he had
better be provided with a vanity like that of Frontinus, or one
more ignoble. If his most desperate concern is to thrust himself
onwards to the top, so that he subscribes in good faith to
Montherlant's formula of '*le combat sans foi*', he will not be
deflected by a temptation to examine values. If he can blow
himself up like a bull-frog with thinking of the organization
that happens to move under him, he will not seek to inquire
whether that organization has any merit apart from the service
it performs to his pride.

[1] Frontinus, *De Aquis Urbis Romae.*

What Administration Is

If Pepys, with his victory over his Committee, and Frontinus with his pomposity and his virtues, display the facts of administration, neither brings us face to face with an explicit theory. They are, however, possibly nearer such a theory than the contemporary writers I have quoted, who seem self-consciously to wish to set on the operation of administration a value which does not belong to it. Miss Cohen with her moral improvement, and Bridges with his artistic delight, have fixed on matters more relevant to other fields than to the one they profess to be describing. The comments which both Bridges and Munro make about the corporate nature of the Civil Servant's work look more hopeful. That indeed is a genuine characteristic but it could not be pretended that it is peculiar to the work of government officials. What J. B. Yeats stigmatizes as the 'collective mind, dull as the House of Commons and serious as the Bank of England'[1] is common to all business transacted in great organizations. It is by an abdication of the individual vision that such organization is possible. There may of course be an individual initiative within such an organization, as there may be an individual initiative or valour within an army, but in so far as an organization exists by meanings rather than by acts there is little place for the sort of individual adjustment of accepted categories which constitutes thought in a properly intellectual field. The adjustments, and the associations and dissociations which are made, are made to suit the necessities and opportunities of action and not to fit the truth which, in any philosophical sense of that term, is irrelevant. 'The practical man', to quote J. B. Yeats again, 'cannot afford to be sincere.'[2] He must, not only on all questions of value but even on matters of fact, share the provisional delusions of his fellows. It is a discipline, but it is not a discipline of the truth. It requires the muscles and obedience of an acrobat rather than the patience of a philosopher.

But because these things are characteristic of all work in a great organization they cannot provide us with a description of the characteristic operation of the official. To find that, we have to look at what distinguishes the administration of government from other forms of collective organization. There is a

[1] J. B. Yeats, *Letters* (1944), p. 239   [2] Yeats, p. 276.

21

tendency more or less plausibly to blur this distinction. It is sometimes even taught that government and industrial organization are closer together than they ever were before, or that government, as Munro contended, now provides services rather than regulations. No doubt it is true that industry presents certain analogies with government, in so far as it requires, as a subordinate purpose, the government of its employees, but an industrial or commercial organization exists for ends of production or commerce which stamp it with its own characteristics. The suggestion of the kinship of industry and government administration is made with the *arrière pensée* that industry will be less hostile to what is said to resemble itself; and so far as the suggestion is believed we have, not an approximation to the truth, but the success of an act of government comparable to the successive acts by which, throughout history, the governor has claimed kinship with the governed in order to secure that he is himself tolerated—a principle which attains its greatest refinement in a complicated modern democracy. This might be called the sympathetic fallacy. Munro's way of describing certain developments in contemporary administration by saying that the official provides not regulation but a service might be called the philanthropic fallacy. This too, so far as it is accepted, represents a triumph of government but not of the truth. For if a government provides a service, it does so for precisely the same reason as it applies a regulation. It does so because it thinks that that is the best way of governing. If you can keep your kingdom quiet with a few policemen armed with battle-axes, your administration can be of the simplest, but if the people will not be quiet without regulations about how it is to pay for its false teeth then even that detail becomes important for the conduct of government. Administration in the present age is characterized by the necessity the administrator may be under of taking notice, because they may become matters of public concern and ultimately of public order, of the most personal concerns. That does not indicate any change in the nature of government; it merely reflects the habits of an urbanized and literate population.

The essential character of government, and so of the administration by which alone it is effective, is a process of maintaining the unity of a political group. This description covers equally the primitive administration of three policemen and, say, the work of an Assistant Secretary in the complicated organization of the welfare state. That is to say, it is a description of the operation of the administrator in both kinds of state as well as in all intermediate kinds of state. Evidently the subject-matter that is put before the administrator may be of the most diverse character, but not the subject-matter or even the weapon, which may be a flint axe-head or a calculating machine, but the aim, constitutes the essence of administration. The administrator steers what may appear to be a craven course among the various pressures of public and still more of semi-public opinion and the opinion of groups, and his concern is to come off with victory, not in the sense that his opinion prevails, for he has no right to one, but in the sense that at the end he is still upright and the forces around him have achieved a momentary balance. Laski regretted that in this country Civil Servants are not to be reckoned among the experts in the subjects with which they deal, that for example no official of the Home Office 'has ever made a contribution of importance to the study of penology or criminology'.[1] That regret shows a mistaken view of the sort of animal the official is. He is, in fact more akin to the criminal than to the criminologist. He is a man who has been trained to a practical operation, not to the expostion of a theory or a search for truth. The operation, in his case, is nothing less than the preservation of the state. He is, no less than any soldier, a man who must give his life to the Crown. That is what gives his task a permanent sense amidst the mutations of party policies.

There is no need for the administrator to be a man of ideas. His distinguishing quality should be rather a certain freedom from ideas. The idealisms and the most vicious appetites of the populace are equal before him. He should be prepared to bow before any wisdom whose mouth is loud enough. It is the negative character of the official's rôle which makes him, while admitted to be honest and trustworthy, an object of distrust. It is clearly undesirable that his cynical method, beneficent in its proper field, should be applied beyond that field. People who, from the official's point of view, are trifling forces at the

[1] Harold J. Laski, *Reflections on the Constitution* (1951), p. 199.

23

periphery of things may, from the point of view of the truth, be at the very centre. The fact that to the administrator they may be of less weight than some less percipient but better organized group should strengthen and not weaken their determination. The acts of the administrator are, in effect, mere acts of recognition. It is the business of those who think they hold the truth on any subject to make themselves recognizable to the administrator's deliberately commonplace vision.

Anything alarming there may be in this description of the administrator's work is due to the generality of the description. Governments differ as countries differ, because the facts to be recognized by them are different. It is the state of society which colours the governments much more than the reverse. Yet government has a certain positive rôle, and those who understand what is being done should use their efforts to secure that the officials are men who might, in the last desperation, exhibit a scruple.

CHAPTER II

The Education of the British Administrator

It might be thought that a profoundly machiavellian, or at any rate jesuitical, education would be required for those who are to stand, as it were, in an empty space in the constitution and advise Ministers while remaining, themselves, stubbornly nothing. In fact, the requirements as to education in the Regulations for the Open Competition for entry into the Administrative Class are extremely modest and could hardly be less specific. There are two methods of entry. For Method I, the Regulations are absolutely silent as to education, though the candidate has to submit to a fairly extensive written examination, for which altogether a thousand marks are allotted as against the further three hundred which are allotted on the strength of an interview before the Final Interview Board. The written examination is made up of:

'(*a*) three compulsory subjects, Essay, English and Present Day, each a maximum of 100 marks;

(*b*) a selection from the optional subjects . . . up to a total of 700 marks. . . .'[1]

As to the compulsory subjects, the Civil Service Commission give these explanations:

'(1) *Essay* (2 hours). One or more general subjects may be set. The object of the essay is to test a candidate's ability to think in general terms, to reason, to set out his thoughts logically and persuasively, and to express himself in good English.

[1] Civil Service Commission: Regulations for recruitment to the Administrative Class of the Home Civil Service, 1958.

(2) *English* (2¼ hours). Candidates will be required to summarize a passage and to answer one of two or three other questions designed to test the understanding and use of English.

(3) *Present Day* (1½ hours). A choice of questions will be given on matters of general interest and importance at the present day—political, social, economic, cultural and scientific. The examiners will look for the intelligent awareness of current affairs which an educated person may be expected to have; good marks will be given for thoughtful opinions and for lucid exposition.'[1]

The optional subjects may, with certain reservations, be chosen at the whim of the candidate from a list which includes most of the menu of Honours degree courses in British universities, so that the Regulations are, in effect, saying nothing as to the subjects the candidate must have studied but merely that he must have followed an Honours course and done well enough to be able to face the competition of other candidates who present themselves. For Method II there is an explicit requirement as to the standard of the candidate's education. It is not exacting:

'Candidates must have, or obtain in 1958, a University degree with first and second class honours.'[2]

The competition under this method does not include a written examination corresponding to that in the optional subjects under Method I. It is as if academic attainments were thought to be sufficiently looked after by the modest requirement as to education. The competition consists of:

'(*a*) A written examination comprising two papers in English, two General Papers, and an Intelligence Test, each with a maximum of 100 marks (making 500 marks in all).

(*b*) A series of tests and interviews at the Civil Service Selection Board.

(*c*) An interview before the Final Selection Board.'[3]

The Civil Service Commission's explanations as to the papers in English, the General Papers and the Intelligence Test are as follows:

[1] Civil Service Commission: General Pamphlet containing information common to the 1958 competitions for the Administrative Class and certain other classes.
[2] Civil Service Commission: Regulations, etc.
[3] Civil Service Commission: Regulations, etc.

'(1) *Essay* (3 hours). For the essay a choice of subjects will be given, based on the main fields of university study (history, languages and civilizations, philosophy, science, social and economic studies, etc.).

Essays should be written for an educated general reader and should not give a narrowly academic or specialist treatment of the subject. Candidates may choose freely what aspects of the subject they will develop and how widely they will range in it but the essay must be relevant to the subject.

In marking the essay examiners will pay special attention to the candidate's grasp of his material and to his ability to think constructively, to reason, and to present his ideas logically and effectively in clear English.

(2) *English* (2¼ hours). Candidates will be required to summarize a passage and to answer one of two or three other questions designed to test the understanding and use of English.

(3). *General Paper* 1 (1½ hours) will be on matters of general interest and importance at the present day—political, social, economic, cultural and scientific . . . [the description is the same as for the Present Day paper under Method I].

(2) *General Paper* 2 (2 hours) will consist of questions devised to test reasoning power, capacity to perceive implications, and ability to distinguish between the important and the less important. One question may involve calculations or the interpretation of graphs and statistics.

(5) *Intelligence Test* (65 minutes). This is a test of mental ability. It consists of short problems involving words, letters and figures; it calls for quick thinking and reasoning, but requires no special knowledge or preparation.'[1]

In their notes on both Method I and Method II the Civil Service Commission have a sentence, the repetition of which suggests what general importance they attach to it, which reads:

'Work in all subjects should be expressed clearly and concisely in good English.'[2]

It is as if it did not matter what one knew as long as one could explain clearly what it was. And this indeed is the sense

---

[1] Civil Service Commission: General Pamphlet, etc.
[2] Civil Service Commission: General Pamphlet, etc.

of the Regulations and the explanatory notes. The Commissioners might be sitting in a drawing-room, so anxious are they to avoid the pedantry of suggesting that anyone should know anything in particular. The candidate has to be able to have 'grasp of his material', 'to think constructively, to reason'. But as to what he is to reason about, let him, as the candidates under Method II are specifically invited to do, 'choose freely what aspects of the subject' already elected by them 'they will develop and how widely they will range in it'. In the Present Day Paper under Method I it is 'intelligent awareness', not, heaven help us, expert knowledge, that is looked for in these future advisers of Ministers, 'thoughtful opinions and lucid exposition', no matter what the thoughts are. The philosophy of the competition finds perfect expression in the words used to describe the Intelligence Test under Method II. 'This', says the explanatory note sublimely, 'is a test of mental ability.'

It is small wonder if, having entered on his career as an administrator through this extraordinarily 'amateur' Open Competition or through the similar, if academically somewhat wider, competition of before the war, the British administrator travelling abroad is shocked to discover that many countries are administered by men who read books about public administration. This, in the British view, is not only a surprising but a very unfortunate state of affairs, and goes some way to explain the disabilities under which foreigners, in the matter of government, notoriously suffer. The British Civil Servant does not want to suppress books of this nature. With his professional tolerance, he is not even altogether against their being read even in this country—by other people. The real turpitude is for people engaged or about to engage in administration to read them. Such people are committing the crime of learning from books something that one just *does*. It is rather like venturing into matrimony only after a course of Havelock Ellis which, for a healthy nature, should not strictly be necessary. Of course the British official appreciates—for no mind is more open than his—that there will always be people who give themselves to such unwholesome studies. They should, he may think, be confined to universities and, preferably, not be allowed to teach.

The Education of the British Administrator

The habits of foreign officials are, on a close acquaintance, more perplexing than ever. Not only do these people read books about administration: they have, in many cases, been admitted to the service only after severe and prolonged academic courses in subjects connected with the theory of government. In this country, on the other hand, administrators are thought of as best trained by apprenticeship, and administration is thought of as something only to be learned by doing it—like riding a bicycle.

It was by no means inevitable that these preconceptions should have won the day. The First Report of Her Majesty's Civil Service Commissioners, published in 1859, has appended to it the text of examination papers, certain of which show that the mind of the examiners was very much on choosing from among the candidates by testing whether they could do the work that was to be done, as well as by eliciting general ability. The examiners did not insist on any particular set of studies relating to law or government having been followed as a preliminary. Had they done so, they would have had to plump for law, as the only formal study of this character then known, and assuredly it was far from their thoughts that a man could not transact public business without having been trained as an attorney. On the other hand, many people at the time would no doubt have been sceptical of the suggestion that proficiency in subjects invented by German philologists—had those subjects then made sufficient progress here to constitute a threat to our educational system—might be the basis of the selection, though Macaulay was in favour of trial by 'Cherokee and astrology' as early as 1833. The Northcote-Trevelyan recommendations, on which the first examination papers were based, certainly opened the way to that sort of thing. The subjects for the examination, said Northcote-Trevelyan, should be 'as numerous as may be found practicable, so as to secure the greatest and most varied amount of talent in the public service.'[1] The authors of that famous report did not, however, have quite our contemporary indifferentism as to the subjects studied. They had in mind ensuring a place for 'history, jurisprudence, political economy, modern languages, political and physical geography,

[1] *Report on the Organization of the Permanent Civil Service, 1854*, p. 14.

and other matters, besides the staple of classics and mathematics,' and they anticipated that there would be some relationship between the subjects taken in the examination and the allocation of the successful candidates, for they spoke of the examination as affording an opportunity for judging in 'what kind of situation' the candidate was 'likely to be most useful.'[1]

Although the papers appended to the First Report of the Commissioners are in the main of a more general kind, some of them contain practical exercises designed directly to test the candidate's aptitude for the work he would find waiting for him:[2]

'Read the following Despatches, etc.' (and then) 'Write a letter to the Lord Commissioners of Her Majesty's Treasury, stating the substance of Lord Grey's original instructions, and the extent to which those instructions were complied with, and the reasons why they were not fully carried out at the time. . . .

' . . . Read the preceding documents, observing carefully the difficulties referred to in the despatch, and the justification which they were considered to afford to the course pursued by the Governor of the Colony.

'Write a clear and explicit answer from the Secretary of State for the Colonies.

'The following heads are given for your letter. . . .

'Give a very short analysis of the Colonial Act (Text supplied). . . .

'N.B. In writing the above letter express at length the reasons which are indicated in the above notes, and add any others which suggest themselves to you.'[3]

Assuredly the candidate who performed these exercises with distinction would not be out of place as a junior assistant to the men whose job it is to advise Ministers and to execute business for them. The test was a practical one—not less so than the more modest test, of the same date, in which the candidate is instructed to copy a paper which was reproduced in

[1] *Report*, etc., *1854*.

[2] Cf: 'It would probably be right to include in the examination some exercises bearing directly upon official business.' (*Report*, etc., p. 14).

[3] *First Report of Her Majesty's Civil Service Commissioners, together with Appendices, 1856*, pp. 115–18, and 130.

handwriting 'correcting the orthography, punctuation, etc. . . .
and all mistakes where necessary and writing abbreviations at
full length.'[1]

A certain acquaintance with the forms and methods of public
business is implied. The best candidate would be one trained
as Sir Henry Taylor, in the 'ironical treatise on the art of
succeeding' which was first published in 1836, suggested that
'The Statesman' should be trained. Taylor's book, which is
of interest still for the information it gives about the conduct
of business in the first half of the nineteenth century as well as
for the general views it contains, is in one matter more realistic
than most later discussions. At many points in his exposition
the author does not trouble to distinguish between the qualifications necessary for the politician and those required by the permanent official. In our day no one is likely to fail to underline the
difference between these two rôles. One reason for this is the
development of democratic theory which makes it near blas-
phemy to mention in the same breath the elected and the un-
elected. Another is the genuine needs of an age of facilitated
communications in which the politician, though not the official,
has to live in a world of newsprint and television, visible to all
like a goldfish in a bowl. But Taylor was mainly concerned with
what was needed for the actual transaction of public business,
and this involves cutting a figure in a more private world of
councils and cabinets, which is, precisely, a world in which the
several rôles of Minister and official are apt to be less sharply
differentiated. Taylor's view was that the pupil who was to un-
dertake state employment should be brought 'closely to matters
of business'.[2] Summary histories, such as Gibbon's, were
thought not to be much good for him; 'materials for histories',
such as the Clarendon state papers, 'rather than the histories
themselves' were the proper study and, when he was ready for
them, the pupil should make use of contemporary parliamentary
publications and other published material of the kind:

'Let a question be selected which has been inquired into by a
committee of either House of Parliament; let the minutes of

[1] *First Report*, etc., 1856, p. 182.
[2] Sir Henry Taylor, *The Statesman: An ironical treatise on the art of succeeding* (1927), p. 6.

evidence taken before the committee be laid before the pupil without their report; and let him be required to report upon that evidence himself, exhibiting, 1st, the material facts of the case as drawn from the evidence; 2nd, the various views and opinions which have been or might be adopted upon the matter; 3rd, the conclusions of his own judgment, with his reasons; 4th, if he concludes for legislation, a draft of the law by which he would execute his purposes; 5th, a draft of the speech with which he would introduce his proposed law to the notice of the legislature.'[1]

The training which would make the pupil ready for these final exercises included acquiring a 'general knowledge of the laws of the land, and of international law, of foreign systems of jurisprudence, and especially a knowledge of the prominent defects of the system at home . . .' and it is added that 'political economy should be taught with equal care'.[2] Taylor is thus suggesting a thorough-going professional training for those who are to engage in public business. And since in his view, which has lost none of its force in spite of the pullulation of committees and the convivial habits of business men, 'business is seldom really and usefully transacted otherwise than in writing',[3] the training is to aim at an unaffected and workmanlike literacy as well as at knowledge of affairs. The examination papers of 1855 assumed the need for the former qualifications and for a knowledge of the specific literary habits of men of affairs. They did not call for the extensive juristic and economic studies which Taylor also recommended. The system might well, on the evidence the papers give of the way people's minds were turning, have developed in such a way as to require such studies. There were good reasons why it could not do so immediately. The education Taylor recommended was not to be had, at any rate in the institutions supposed to provide education. Taylor himself had been educated by browsing in his father's library, and it is doubtful whether, there, he undertook the studies he later recommended to others. In any case he was probably not thinking of the curricula of schools and universities. His recommendations are those of a man who has spent some years in a public office and then pauses

[1] Taylor, p. 6.   [2] Taylor, p. 5.   [3] Taylor, p. 35.

to devise, for those who come into the business after him, a training which he himself has been spared. They are akin to the advices which gentlemen used to give their sons as to how to prepare themselves for a career at court, advice which nobody would follow but which tells one something about the nature of the life it relates to. When the first Civil Service examination papers were set in 1855 undergraduates at Oxford and Cambridge might study classics or mathematics. The history schools were not in full vigour there till about 1870; the craze for public administration at the London School of Economics dates from the late nineties; Marshall's Economics Tripos at Cambridge from about the turn of the century; and the Oxford School of Politics, Philosophy and Economics from after the First World War.

Yet even now that studies akin to those recommended by Taylor for his statesman flourish or at least prevail in a number of universities, and are admitted by the Civil Service Commissioners to be no less useful, for those who are to enter the higher ranks of the Service, than Old High German or astronomy, the number of entrants who have followed such studies is not overwhelming.[1] Such recruits are not, in the eyes of the service, either more or less qualified, by reason of their studies, than those who spent their time on studies apparently with less direct relationship to their future employment. That such studies are not required, or specially regarded where they have been undertaken, may, to the foreigner accustomed to other practices, or to a few university people who cherish Taylorian theories, seem odd. But it is not fortuitous. It is connected with a certain reading of the nature of public administration, one which has come naturally in a country where, until at any rate the end of the eighteenth century, the bulk of the administration was in the hands of magistrates, whose great qualification was to have no special qualification but to be reputable, unlearned and in every way ordinary.

There are, in the Civil Service itself, those who would like to see a slightly more theoretical briskness in the British administrator. A notable apologist for this point of view is E. N.

---

[1] Of the 39 candidates who succeeded in the Administrative Competition in 1957, 6 had studied Economics or Politics, Philosophy and Economics and 2 had studied Law. There were 8 Historians.

Gladden, who appears to view the Administrative Class with disapproval on a number of grounds. One should not be put off by the false antinomy with which he introduces an interesting discussion of the place of theory in the official's training. 'Whether administration is an art or a skill with which a person is endowed at birth, as some would like to maintain, or a science calling for all the abilities of the scholar. . . .'[1] The former alternative is full of the echoes of romanticism, but it has in fact never been suggested that the administrator was a sort of noble savage. The dispute is rather whether there is some sort of 'science', some specific academic discipline, which is an indispensable preliminary to effective functioning as an administrator or whether, on the other hand, the formula of *nascitur atque fit* is not best satisfied by picking an intelligent young man or woman, who has had a good non-vocational education, and subjecting him or her to the moral and intellectual discipline of apprenticeship in an office where the affairs of government are transacted. 'We have not yet adjusted our minds to the fact that administration now calls for knowledge of complex processes which cannot be understood without a close and prolonged study. The administrative leaders in general . . . reinforce the cult of ignorance by regarding administration as a mysterious preserve upon which no self-elected outsider should be encouraged to trespass. . . .'[2] The mystery, however, can hardly be said to be on the side of the hard-boiled administrator. What he is saying is simply that the business of his office is best understood by someone who, like himself, is at the point where political intentions and executive requirements meet. No man of affairs works less secretly than the public administrator since none has so often to explain publicly what he is about. It is hardly proof of the existence of a mystery cult if he chooses to doubt whether there is about his job anything of general and permanent importance which can be taught *a priori* in addition to the *ad hoc* explanations which are demanded all the time by M.P.s and others. That public business is often complicated no one who has engaged in it would be disposed to deny, but what are the 'complex processes' in general, as distinct from those

[1] E. N. Gladden, *The Essentials of Public Administration* (1953), p. 211.
[2] Gladden, p. 212.

belonging to a particular job or a particular piece of business, and which can usefully be the object of 'close and prolonged study', is much more doubtful. No subject matter is more elusive than that of administrative studies, in the sense of studies which can be seen by people engaged in the job to be relevant to it. That indeed might be called a 'mysterious preserve'. Gladden does not do much to enlighten us as to its content; perhaps he means no more than that the Civil Servant should be made to study the structure of governmental organization. It is of interest that, enthusiastic as he is for administrative studies, Gladden does not adopt the extreme course of suggesting a special preliminary education for those who are entering the public service, but contents himself with suggesting 'a course of professional studies' after entry. There would be certificates, and diplomas, and no one would be promoted without them, but exactly what he would have studied, and why, is not altogether clear. The objects Gladden, like a good Britisher, has in mind, are strictly practical, and his course would perhaps hardly contain the material that would enable the British official to engage in high-brow conversation with his continental brother. It has to be borne in mind that Gladden is using 'administration' in a wide sense, to cover almost all the activities of the Civil Service, whereas we have been more concerned with activities and point of view of those whom he calls 'administrative leaders'. For the latter, one might reasonably fear a training which would enable them to 'approach a new project as an expert who knows most of the answers'.[1]

In practice the new entrant into the Administrative Class is inducted rather than trained. He is not required to follow anything that could be called a course of study—nothing, certainly, that would come up to the Gladden standard; nor is what he is taught of the kind that consumes the youth of the continental administrative lawyer. Indeed one may say that he is shown what happens rather than introduced to a corpus of theory or of law. His main teachers are those preoccupied men, the principals in whose divisions he is put to serve. The principal will be concerned with some modest part of his Minister's affairs. Characteristically, he will have a staff of executives who know

[1] Gladden, p. 212.

the details of the business and have grown wise in the service, and as the greenest but, it should be, not the least intelligent of this staff the new recruit will see what befalls the correspondence that comes to the division and should learn the sort of considerations which govern its fate. Some of the correspondence will be internal; some will come from individual members of the public; some from the innumerable groups and associations which jostle around government departments; and some will be from Members of Parliament. Each kind will have its several use for the instruction of the newcomer. There will be Parliamentary Questions, and the recruit may be asked to try his hand at drafting replies, if only to see what inventions of their own his betters prefer to his draft. There will be other occasional parliamentary matters, and Hansard will come round to him each day so that he can see how his Minister is faring. He will learn the art and use of minute writing—and reading—and attend meetings of varying degrees of usefulness. After about six months he will be moved to another job, and after that to another, learning in time what administration is by seeing methods, habits and hunches applied to a variety of subject-matters between them, ultimately, a series of connections appear. In some cases there will be visits or even a period of apprenticeship outside London.

Before the war this practical introduction to the work he had to do was the only form of training of the new entrant that was attempted. Since the war, the practice of showing the recruit around a variety of jobs has possibly been somewhat more systematized. Certainly the scope has been extended and the assistant principal may now spend two or three weeks of his training period abroad. Moreover, when he is first posted to a Ministry he will probably attend a short training course which has been devised mainly for executive recruits and after a few months service he will spend a fortnight at a Treasury course which is attended by assistant principals from all Ministries. The latter course is small—some sixteen or eighteen strong— and is drawn from candidates who have entered the Administrative Class after service in the Executive or Clerical Class as well as the young men and women direct from universities. The main object of the course is to show the recruit, who has in his own Ministry already begun to see what Civil Service work is like, something of the wider context into which the work of his Department fits. The talks are given by senior civil servants and by visitors from outside the service. A senior or junior Minister is invited to speak on each course. The whole scheme is modest and practical and by its modesty serves to emphasize the principle of the British service that the administrative officer's training throughout his career comes from his actual work on the tasks to which he is assigned. 'This practice', to quote an authoritative Treasury source, 'is in accordance with the long-established tradition of regarding members of the Administrative Class as intelligent amateurs who form their judgments on the basis of experience rather than as a result of a prescribed course of theoretical training.'

CHAPTER III

The Training of the Administrator in Germany and France

No doubt in all countries responsible officials are people 'who form their judgments on the basis of experience'. By the time responsibility descends on them they are some years from their theoretical training. But what they have forgotten remains of some significance in relation to their general attitudes and habits of work. It represents the direction in which they were launched, and that direction is not fortuitous, but is determined by constitutional considerations which have a permanent importance for their work. In the British conception, it would be better if the administrator did not exist at all. He does in fact exist and cannot be wished away, but at least his education and training are such as are appropriate to a man who is supposed to have no pretensions to play a positive rôle. He merely serves his Minister, and since his Minister lives by satisfying the House of the reasonableness and common sense of what he does the administrator who serves him is a man whose characteristic interest is in the intelligibility of what is done, or rather in its explicability in terms Parliament will accept. Hence the insistence in the Open Competition on the capacity to understand and explain things rather than on the possession of any particular body of knowledge, and the avoidance in the scheme for training new entrants of anything which would suggest to them that they could become experts who, as Gladden would have it, would 'know most of the answers'. The character of the British system is seen more clearly if one considers the conception of the qualifications and training of the administrator which prevails on the European mainland. On this matter there

The Training of the Administrator

really is something like a 'European view' with which our own may be contrasted; and our practice is seen to be singular. In general, the continental administrator, of the type which corresponds more or less to our Administrative Class, is a lawyer, specializing in that branch of law—namely administrative law—which is most directly concerned with the function of government. If he has no former legal qualifications—which is comparatively rare—he is likely to have undertaken formal studies in some other subject—such as economics—of the kind supposed, in our time, specially to promote an understanding of the works of government.

The German system of training recruits to the administration is clearly set in the framework of ordinary legal training. A young man may not, as with us, follow his bent in literature or philosophy until the moment of graduation and then decide that he will have a shot at getting into the public service. The first decision he must have made, when he started his career as a student, is to study law. At this stage he need not commit himself further. When he has taken his first state examination[1] in law, at the age of about twenty-three, he may go on for three and a half years as a sort of legal apprentice under the care of the Ministry of Justice of one of the constituent states of the Federation. He then takes the second state examination.[2] So far his course has been one which would equip him equally to be a judge, an administrator, or to be otherwise employed in legal practice, and it is only at this stage that he has to plump, if he wants to do so, for the public service. He is by now aged twenty-six or twenty-seven, and if he enters the public service he has still three years probation to do before he receives a permanent appointment as an official.

The man who thus enters the public service, at the age of twenty-six or seven, will have considerably less practical knowledge of administration than the British assistant principal who, at that age, may have spent three or four years in the service. The German's practical experience will be limited, generally, to a brief period during his three and a half years, as a

[1] The so-called *Referendar* examination, taken after three or three and a half years (6 or 7 semesters) of legal studies.
[2] The *Assessor* examination.

The Training of the Administrator

Referendar, between the first and second state examinations in law. As little as a sixth of the time as *Referendar* may be devoted to administrative training[1] and although some of that training will be practical, three or four months of it are likely to be spent at the School of Administration in Speyer.

The school in Speyer was originally designed by the French authorities to train officials for work in their zone. With the establishment of the Federal Republic it was thrown open to officials from all parts of Western Germany. The school is not, however, a direct dependency of the Bonn Government. In the Federal Republic things are not so simple. The charter of the school in its present form is a law passed in 1950 by the Parliament of Rheinland-Pfalz, in which state Speyer is situated, but the institution is run in accordance with an agreement—to which Bonn is also a party—between the member states of the Federation. Although it is mainly concerned with people who are to make their careers in the higher branches of the public services of the states of the Federation, eligibility is not confined to such people, since it is only after the second state examination, as *Assessor* and not as *Referendar*, that people are admitted to the higher ranks of the public service, and the main courses at Speyer are for the *Referendar*. In the earlier legal study public law will not have occupied the major part of the syllabus; at Speyer it is the main if not the only thing. The list of courses from which the student has to choose includes, it is true, an item on private law and certain courses of a general character on economics, sociology and history. The only compulsory course, however, is one in administration and administrative law, and though the students, through an anxiety to show the width of their interests or a mere weariness with the law, do go in considerable numbers to the general courses the shadow of the second state examination is there and the most earnest efforts must go into courses directly useful for it. The authorities feel that mere preparation for the second examina-

[1] The proportion of the *Referendar* time devoted to administrative training varies as between one *Land* and another, but it nowhere exceeds a third and is generally considerably less. The training before entry into the service is thus emphatically that of a lawyer, and the importance attached to administrative training is not very great. See: Erich Becker, *Entwicklung und Aufgaben der Hochschule für Verwaltungswissenschaften Speyer* (issued by the School), p. 27.

tion does not play too large a part in the activities of the school, but it is significant that, while students may hear an admirable and intelligent course of lectures introducing them to the mysteries of sociology, and may in that connection or another spend a good deal of time on discussions of non-legal matters, the written work is mainly of a legal character, though it includes some work in economics.

There are three main forms of activity in the school in addition to the lectures, which are themselves so conducted as to allow a considerable time for discussion, though as they are attended by anything from thirty to a hundred students it is to be presumed that only the more enterprising take part in it. There is the seminar, to which between twenty and forty students go, and at which they have in turn to open a discussion of some problem listed in the syllabus. There is the syndicate, with thirty to forty-five members, at which case studies are considered. Lastly, there is the written exercise. For the syndicates and the written exercises the school does not have to rely on its imagination. For every course, there is a flow of sample cases from the various states, and in a country with some hundred and thirty Ministries there is no reason why this stream should ever dry up, though the immediate sources are only the Ministries of the Interior of the various states and the administrative courts. We are far here from the fantasy of some American case-studies, some of which are written up as a sort of administrative science fiction.[1] We are also some distance from the practice of administration, though less far, no doubt, from the German practice than from our own. What we have is so many legal problems, illustrated where necessary by documents, and what is asked for is perhaps a draft judgment or a legal opinion. Indeed we have something very like the training recommended by Taylor ('The Statesman') but, so to speak, in a more barren field. Whereas Taylor wanted practical

[1] The reader who is curious as to this form of literature, which will no doubt have a place in history among the less exhilarating literary curiosities of the age, may conveniently look at Harold Stein's *Public Administration and Policy Development: a case book* (New York, 1952). One object of such studies is indicated by Stein's sentence (p. xiv): 'Thorough understanding of public administration is possible only for those who are willing to undergo *at least vicariously* the pangs of decision.' (My italics.)

suggestions as to the best way to settle some problem of the kind that Ministers and advisory committees have to wrestle with, the manifest concern in these exercises at Speyer is that the student shall not think outside the crabbed circle of the law. That preoccupation is perhaps partly to be explained by the bitter experience of abuse of power, and by the conditions of work in a service in which there is a certain lack of trust between Ministers and officials, and a certain degree of consequential paralysis on the part of the officials.

There was a time when officials without academic training, who had been promoted from below, were admitted to Speyer. Since 1952 there have been none. It may be imagined how their presence threatened the pretensions of Speyer to be a higher establishment for the teaching of public law. One does not gather, however, that the staff disliked these intruders; on the contrary, they speak highly of their performance. But the feeling against such people is stronger than can be imagined in a service like ours where, outside the technical branches, nobody gives a thought to a man's academic qualifications once he has been recruited. In the British Imperial Calendar the names of officials stand unembellished by anything save an indication of their rank and function and any honours they have earned—normally in the service. In the German list there stands beside the name the date when the official took the second state examination in law, and the dash which replaces that entry if he did not is a branding with a social as well as an academic significance attached to it. It is not suggested that any considerable accession of strength would accrue to the German service through the admittance to Speyer of people without academic qualifications. No doubt in Germany, as elsewhere, only the rare man of outstanding merit who had missed university training through some accident would be suitable for higher posts, and the output of universities is such that such men must in the future be much rarer than in the past.

The school at Speyer illustrates extremely well the continental view of what the qualifications and training of the administrator should be. There is of course much in the school, and more in the general scheme of training, which is specifically German. The school's origin as a place for training administrators for the French zone has left little trace on its character, which has mainly been formed by the forces which are at work in the German administration itself. None the less, and for the very reason that the German administration, in spite of all its national peculiarities, conforms in its general outline to a general European pattern, Speyer shows us what our idiosyncrasies are. The fact that the German scheme is so closely tied to legal training—more, perhaps, than the authorities of the school themselves would choose—throws our amateurishness into the sharpest relief. In the French scheme there is a stronger, at first sight almost British, emphasis on practice. Indeed certain aspects of the scheme are said to have been in part inspired by the British model though, just as the French origins of the Speyer school were soon lost in the stronger national element, so any British ideas there may once have been in the French scheme have been gallicized beyond recognition.

The French scheme of training centres around the *Ecole Nationale d'Administration* in Paris. The aspirations which attended the founding of that institution are indicated in an order dated 9 October 1945 and in the *Exposé des Motifs* accompanying it.[1] the documents in which, in accordance with French practice and habits of thought, a beginning was made by 'hastily fixing on paper some fine theoretical constructions'[2] (by contrast with the British method, which a French student of the subject confesses to be 'more prudent', of allowing legislative reform to follow the evolution of facts and ideas). 'The training of young people', runs the *Exposé*, 'who are destined for the higher cadres of the service' is incomplete; the *Ecole libre des Sciences politiques* is at present the only institution to offer a systematic programme of courses and lectures as a preparation for the higher ranks of the service; it is practically speaking open only to well-off students living in Paris. Our universities do not give a large enough place to the teaching of the social and political sciences. . . .' That is not the sort of complaint one hears among British administrators discussing

[1] The text of the order and the *Exposé des Motifs* is given in the brochure entitled *Concours et Scolarité*, 1956, issued by the *École Nationale d'Administration*, p. 169.

[2] Gilbert Tixier, *La Formation des Cadres supérieurs de l'Etat en Grande-Bretagne et en France* (1948), p. 53.

recruitment to their service. The *Exposé* was, however, in effect blessing an established French predilection for regarding administration as something the elements of which can be learnt academically. It may well be extravagant to claim that the British Civil Servant is a gentleman; but if that description were accepted, if only by way of tribute to the vagueness of his qualifications, then the French Civil Servant must be regarded, on the lines of Montaigne's distinction, as a kind of grammarian. The French administrator has in general (we are concerned here with the higher ranks only) had a specialized academic training, and is a creature of the law, by virtue of his training, as indeed in other respects. The immense majority of France's administrators come from the law faculties or from other institutions which address themselves to the teaching of law or of such subjects as economics, sociology and political science. Before the war candidates for the *Conseil d'Etat* had as a preliminary to obtain their *licence en droit*. But this was a minimum requirement. They were also recommended to acquire the diploma of the *Ecole libre des Sciences politiques*. The background of the candidates for other posts of comparable importance was not very different. In this academic context it is perhaps not surprising that, when a reform of the recruitment and training of the French administration took place it involved the creation of another school. At the same time, however, as the *Exposé* by implication blessed the established predilection for regarding administration as something with a grammar which could be academically learnt, it demonstrated an uneasiness about the extent and nature of the existing specialization inside the service. It drew attention to the limitations arising from separate recruitment—which, in contrast with our own general competition for the Administrative Class, had always been the French practice—for 'the *Conseil d'Etat*, the civil staff of the central administrations' and other bodies 'at the very heart of the public services'.[1] What the authors of the *Exposé* envisaged, therefore, was a continuation, even a certain hardening, of the basic French tradition as to the nature of administration, but at the same time the injection into it of the notion that this specialized activity was of much the same kind whether it went

[1] *Concours et Scolarité*, p. 169.

on in one department of government or another. With this latter notion went a desire for a clearer distinction than had hitherto existed in France between the work of what we should call the administrative and the executive grades, the creation of appropriate cadres (the '*administrateurs civils*' and the '*secrétaires d'administration*'), and the establishment of a *Direction de la Fonction publique* and a *Conseil permanent de l'Administration civile*, which were designed to make a common policy possible and effective.[1] There was therefore an element of far-reaching reform in what was proposed. Moreover, the new school which was to be set up was in certain respects to be unlike the traditional French educational establishment. '*Elle s'efforcera*'—and the verb indicates what a wrench it would be—'to develop in the candidates a feeling for the high duties of the public service and give them the means to carry out those duties well.'[2]

Admission to the school was to be—and has effectively been —by one of two competitions. The first competition is designed for graduates about to begin their careers; for these candidates, entry into the school is at the same time recruitment into the Civil Service. The upper age limit for this competition is twenty-six. The second competition, for which the age limits are twenty-four to thirty, is for candidates already in the service; it is a condition of entry that one should have had at least four years' service. For this competition no academic qualifications are required, but the statistics for 1955[3] show that while a relatively small number of candidates *sans diplôme* did in fact attempt the competition, none succeeded. A substantial number of candidates armed only with the *baccalauréat* made a brave assault, but all but one were repulsed. For the rest, the candidates were of the classic type, though qualifications additional to the *licence en droit* were commoner in the first competition, which might be taken as evidence of a modest victory for a policy, which was among the explicit aims of the authors of the *Exposé*, of opening the way to the *jeunes gens sans fortune*.[4]

---

[1] This reform was not completely carried out.   [2] *Concours et Scolarité*, p. 170.
[3] *École Nationale d'Administration: Epreuves et Statistiques des Concours de* (1955), p. 154.
[4] Many candidates in the second competition who had higher degrees obtained them after finishing their full-time studies and while working in the Service. This also suggests that those *sans fortune* have had some success.

The Training of the Administrator

The written tests for entry were indeed of such a nature as inevitably to exclude people without academic qualifications. One does not see many young men, by the light of nature, acquiring the ability to write, to the satisfaction of French examiners, a composition of six hours 'on a subject, relating to the general evolution of political, economic or social ideas or events since the end of the eighteenth century', to say nothing of three or four more tests or essays of four hours apiece. Nor, for that matter does one see him standing up to a jury which, in the oral tests, does nothing less than 'take the exact measure of the candidate'—an operation which can hardly be performed on anybody except in accordance with some pretty rigidly preconceived notions, especially when one bears in mind that there is here question, not of a drawing-room interview, which the traditional tensions between examiner and examined would render difficult in France, but of a commentary on a text presented to the candidate.

The course at the school lasts three years, and is made up of:

'— one year of external training or *dépaysement*, at a prefecture or in North Africa;

'— one year of study at the school, made up of general instruction, specialized work . . . language courses, physical education and military training.

'— one year made up firstly, of a training period in private industry, then a cycle of instruction, practical work, . . . and time spent in administrative offices, designed . . . for apprenticeship as much as for information.'[1]

It is clear that the conception of training represented by the school is far from being merely academic. Great importance is attached to the initial training at a prefecture, which is certainly the best possible place for the young graduate to acquire a general knowledge of French administration and the place where he least risks losing himself in the by-ways of specialist interests. One may feel that the claims made for this '*stage de dépaysement*' are even a little melodramatic. These periods are: 'destined to put the student in touch with human reality, to show him the working of an *administration d'autorité*. and to

[1] *Concours et Scolarité*, p. 34.

enable him to measure himself against the daily difficulties and risks of the job. . . . They demand from the trainee . . . the qualities that will be expected of him later on . . . an enquiring mind, firmness of character, and that sense of the human which should always inform and temper authority. . . .'[1] A good deal of time in the second year is given to courses the object of which must be to add to the candidate's knowledge rather than, directly, to improve his ability to act, and to remove any doubt as to the academic nature of those studies they are described by the school as amounting to a '*doctorat supérieur.*'[2] It is in the first year and last year that the procedures of the school approach most closely to the Anglo-Saxon conception of an institution designed to train people to perform tricks rather than one designed to inculcate learning. There can be no doubt of the value, to the student who is both intelligent and diligent, of these periods. The time spent, at the end of the course, outside the service, is probably taken fairly light-heartedly. The student already has his final classification (though not the order of his nomination to the new cadre) when he starts it. The initial *stage* is another matter. As a graduate in law or some allied subject, the student already has some theoretical knowledge of what he will find in and about the prefecture. If he comes from the second competition he will, of course, already have had some practical experience of the government service. In either case he may be supposed to be less lost than an assistant principal who has devoted his academic career to the study of Anglo-Saxon or Greek. The value of the *stage*, however, must largely depend on the men at the prefecture. Some prefectures already have in place men who have come out of the school. They may be supposed to understand the requirements of the *stagiaire*, and to help him to make the best use of his time. In some prefectures, however, there is probably little attempt to understand what the newcomer needs; there is even some feeling against the 'competition wallahs' recruited through *E.N.A.*, and in such an atmosphere he will be given some odd jobs but otherwise thrown much on his own resources.

[1] *Concours*, etc., pp. 34–5.
[2] It is only fair to add, however, that many of the lectures at the School are given by active officials, who deal with their subjects from a practical point of view.

The Training of the Administrator

He has, during his period at the prefecture, to complete a *'mémoire de stage'* on a subject set by the school. The subject is by way of a report on some of the services he will come into contact with. It would seem that this exercise, like much that is done in the second year at the school, is somewhat too abstract, too like the abstract study of institutions to which the student is already accustomed. It is true that this time the candidate is looking at the services themselves and not merely reading about them. But administrative work in practice rarely gives occasion or opportunity for a *general* look at a service. In administration there is no such thing as the note written without specific purposes. The terms of reference, the things to be looked for, are determined by the nature of the decisions which have to be taken, by the status and function of the person for whom the note is written, and by the political and personal atmosphere of the moment. An assistant principal who is put to draft Private Office letters is being shown the meaning of such terms of reference; the *stagiaire* who has to produce a *mémoire* is not.

A former pupil of the *Ecole Nationale* wrote, of the emphasis on *knowledge* which is so characteristic of that establishment and so uncharacteristic of the British machinery for recruiting administrators: 'In this land of jurists, such a development was not desirable, but it could have been foreseen. It tends to do away with the originality of the experiment or at any rate to make it less, and to bring us back to the traditions of the specialized competition. . . . *E.N.A.*, in the end, flatters and magnifies the dreams of the *fonctionnaire* but it does not change them.'[1]

[1] *Promotions (revue fondée par les élèves de l'E.N.A.)* No. 38.

CHAPTER IV

Administrator and Law in France

The emphasis which both the school in Speyer and the *Ecole Nationale*, in spite of the more comprehensive conceptions of the latter, put on legal qualifications and training, reflects certain characteristics common to the French and German Civil Services and, indeed to European Civil Services in general. These common characteristics are in part a consequence of the prevalence over most of Europe of the traditions of Roman Law and consequently of the passion for codification. More immediately they are due to Napoleon, and one cannot travel around Europe looking at her bureaucracies without receiving the strongest impression of Napoleon's administrative force, even though one may also reflect on the different thing his works became when that force had departed. Perhaps it would not be putting too sharp a point on the matter to say that one sees the importance, for the British Civil Service, of the Battle of Trafalgar. Certainly the French Civil Service is in some sense the type and pattern of modern European bureaucracies, and there are important differences in kind between most of those bureaucracies and our own.

The typical guide-book to the British Civil Service is a descriptive work which sets out at more or less length what the various Ministries are supposed to *do*. The starting point for the study of the French service, on the other hand, is almost inevitably a legal text-book. It is no longer permitted to say that we have no administrative law, but most British administrators would find it difficult to say what it is.

> *With cow and plough and barley mow*
> *We puzzle all our brains.*

The merest aspirant to the French service could tell you precisely:

'It is merely a branch of public law. It is concerned with the state and the state's relations with individuals. It is made up of the whole body of rules relating to the organization and working of the public services and the relations of those services with private persons.'[1]

Though the present French administration derives much of its form from the Napoleonic reorganization of the year VIII, its spirit is distinctly not that of the Consulate, and the relationship of the *administré* to the state is very different from what it then was. The First Consul made use of the revolutionary principle of the subordination of the administration to the law because such principles were part of the material of government in his day, but the *administré* had no guarantees against arbitrary treatment and the state was irresponsible. The administrative law on which French Civil Servants are now nursed, and which they spend their days manipulating or complicating, is by contrast a tissue of rights and privileges accorded to the citizen. It is explicitly conceived of as setting limits not merely to the actions of officials, but of Ministers who, it is feared, might without this restraint 'let party considerations prevail in the execution of their administrative tasks'.[2] Its characteristic organ is the *Conseil d'Etat*, the most prominent function of which now is to act as a supreme administrative court to which the *administré* may have recourse in his battle against administrator and government. The evolution of the last hundred and fifty years, which has brought the *Conseil d'Etat* to this position, has likewise effected a fundamental change in the position of the official. In the system of the year VIII, officials were conceived of as performing only preparatory and executive work; it was the Minister who took the decision. In time the officials came 'to want to be something else than subordinates without guarantees and without initiative'.[3] Louis Rolland's explanation of this change conveys in few words weighty indications as to the nature of the French system:

'The officials had reason to complain of arbitrary treatment

---

[1] Louis Rolland, *Précis de Droit administratif* (1957), p. 1.
[2] Rolland, p. 6.　　　　　[3] Rolland, p. 8.

and favouritism on the part of the Ministers at the head of the services. The abuses became all the more apparent since the number of services and, consequently, of officials continually went on growing, the suffrage was extended and the parliamentary régime was installed. A Minister, whose position depends on the votes of a majority, is inclined to secure the votes of the deputies by satisfying the demands they make regarding the officials in their constituencies.'[1]

To remedy or mitigate these abuses, and for more general social reasons, the officials were in time given important guarantees. The status of French officials is regulated by a law of 19 October 1946. Alain Plantey, in his *Traité pratique de la Fonction publique*, says that 'the situation of the members of the French service is now thought of as objectively determined by the legislative and regulatory dispositions taken by the administrative authorities . . .' and that 'these rules being fixed, once for all, do not need the agreement of those concerned before they are applied. . . . The theory most generally applied is that of the statute: officials, established or not, are in an objective legislative and regulatory situation.'[2] That is magnificent language: its practical meaning is that the legal definitions of the official's position place him in an artificial position of great strength. His rights have been written up in such complicated fashion that it is difficult for those who would otherwise be in a position to manage him to do so. Plantey himself puts the matter almost as brutally: 'the statutory character of the legal régime . . . has as its principal consequence the rigidity of the administrative structures, automatic working, the absence of new methods and outlooks. Indeed, the object of the statute is to protect the official and the service against the arbitrary intervention of political power; but that object is soon over-reached; the authorities in the hierarchy are thus deprived of their power; responsibilities are watered down, rewards no longer go by merit, and the permanence of the employment, for all but the highest officials, makes way for all kinds of negligence. . . .'[3] For the official himself, the statutory basis means that he has a legal vested interest in whatever

[1] Rolland, p. 8   [2] Alain Plantey: *Traité de la Fonction publique* (1956), p. 15.
[3] Plantey, p. 99.

51

benefits come his way, whether they be in the matter of promotion, establishment or leave. It is not always understood, says Plantey, that officials 'invoke the rights they have acquired under existing regulations against any new regulations which may be less favourable.'[1] No doubt that is, in principle, what British officials do, when they get the chance, and the employees of private enterprise as well. But there is one basic and vital difference. The rights of the British official are, in general, not guaranteed to him by law. Even where the right has a statutory basis, as is the case with superannuation, the law in fact merely gives a discretionary power to the Treasury. It is the Treasury who determine the amount of the pension, if any, which is to be granted, and no one has any reason to doubt that they will do so in accordance with the rules promulgated. But the retiring Civil Servant dissatisfied with the amount, alleging, perhaps, that not all of his reckonable service has been taken into account, cannot seek redress either in the ordinary courts nor before any special tribunal such as the *Conseil d' Etat*. The *rights* of the British Civil Servant are minimal, while his duties are clear. In place of rights he has, however, two advantages—a reasonable confidence that the Treasury, although mean, will not actually try to cheat him of his due, and a deeply ingrained habit of negotiation.

In speaking in general terms of the administration, Plantey lays stress on its spirit of hierarchy and centralization. He quotes in the introduction to his book certain words of Michel Debré: 'The administration of modern France was thought out twice, first by Richelieu and then by Napoleon.'[2] Napoleon set out to create a civil hierarchy analogous to the military power, and to the ecclesiastical power which impressed him so much and which is, after all, the pattern of bureaucratic power in modern Europe. The traces of his aspiration remain. Plantey says a little wrily that the duty of obedience to superiors 'is indispensable even in political *régimes* where the accent is not put on hierarchy'.[3] Naturally this duty is written into the statute at several points. Just as naturally, no such thought has ever troubled the heads of British legislators. In spite of the insistence of the French statute on obedience, and in spite of the fact

[1] Plantey, p. 100.   [2] Plantey, p. 7.   [3] Plantey, p. 172.

that 'from the year VIII and throughout almost the whole of
the nineteenth century, the accent was put on the duties of
officials and their narrow hierarchical subordination to the
government', the principle of hierarchic obedience 'has however acquired an increasing number of limitations which'—
and there is, to a foreigner, a touching faith in certain popular
French abstractions behind this last phrase—'are to be taken
for granted in a legal system which, like ours, demands a refined solution of the problem of conciliating the supremacy of
law and the exigencies of the public service, which are bound up
with the ideas of the political régime.'[1] The refinements in
question are very largely the work of the *Conseil d'Etat*. 'All
decisions effecting the official's career' may be brought to that
august body. Nominations, promotions, reversions, disciplinary
penalties, 'can all be attacked in this way'.[2] Judging by the
volume of business before the *Conseil d'Etat*, a very large
number are so attacked. One has the picture of officials watching
one another's careers like lynxes and at each suspicion of an
arguable irregularity in effect going to law about it. It was not
always so. At the end of the last century little besides certain
disciplinary penalties could be treated in this way.

The *Conseil d'Etat*, this most symptomatic of French administrative institutions, has found a brilliant student and an
enthusiastic admirer in C. J. Hamson. It is hardly too much to
say that the book in which he records his findings and his
admiration, *Executive Discretion and Judicial Control*, is a master-
piece. It is brief and lucid, and presents a vivid picture. It is
however to be suspected that it was intended to be, not merely
a study of a foreign institution, but a blow struck in a domestic
quarrel. For Hamson believes profoundly in the justice of the
quarrel which many British lawyers have long engaged in
against the administration in this country, and Hamson sees in
the *Conseil d'Etat* a control of an effectiveness undreamed of
here. The lectures were given under the terms of the Hamlyn
Trust, and Hamson has had to impart an irony, for which he
makes an ingenious apology, into the words of the deed, for
Miss Hamlyn's intent was that 'the Common People of the
United Kingdom may realize the privileges which in law and

[1] Plantey, p. 176.   [2] Plantey, p. 363.

53

custom they enjoy in comparison with other European peoples'.[1] The privileges in this field turn out, in Hamson's view, to be, in comparison with those enjoyed by the French, negative.

Hamson is concerned with 'the judicial business of the *Conseil d'Etat*, the *contentieux administratif*' . . . and within the judicial sphere what interests him most is the '*recours en annulation pour excès de pouvoir*'.[2] In effect he is concerned with the blows which the *Conseil d'Etat* is able to strike against the bogey of lawyers, the executive. Hamson is anxious to assure us that what the *Conseil d'Etat* does in ensuring 'a decent standard'[3] is 'as much in the interests of that administration as in the interests of the individual', and that the work is in fact carried out by what is in effect an administrative *corps d'élite* so that there is no question of rulings being given without knowledge of the needs and rigours of the administrative game. It is no doubt the case that the members of the *Conseil d'Etat* are better equipped for incursions into the administrative field than the generality of lawyers who have learned their trade in and around the courts. The question of interest, however, is not *who* fulfils the peculiar rôle of the *Conseil d'Etat*, but what that rôle is and how it looks from the administrator's, as distinct from the lawyer's piont of view.

Waline, one of the great authorities on administrative law at whose feet Hamson sat, so described the procedure of *recours pour excès de pouvoir*: 'any interested party can ask the administrative tribunal to annul any illegal decision taken by the administrator . . . the appellant simply asks for the disappearance of a record . . . any administrative record which has the character of a decision being susceptible of being annulled.'[4] The disappearance of an *acte* of the administrator! Second best, no doubt, to the final disappearance of the executive, but still a conjuring trick to please a lawyer. Waline, from whom Hamson no doubt takes his line, insists that this trick is 'in the interests

---

[1] C. J. Hamson, *Executive Discretion and Judicial Control* (1954), pp. ix–x.

[2] Hamson, p. 7. The reforms effected in the *Conseil d'État* since Hamson made his inquiries, and which resulted in a measure of decentralization (which cannot have been premature since there was, in February 1953, a back-log of 24,000 cases), do not affect the subject of the following pages.

[3] Hamson, p. 126.

[4] Marcel Waline, *Traité élementaire de droit administratif* (1950), p. 105.

of good administration', and an ingenious Spanish theorist, the Marques de las Marismas[1] makes out that it is itself a kind of administration—a special sort to which he gives the delightful title of '*la Administración vigilante*', in contradistinction to '*la Administración actuante*', which is what most people think administration is. Marismas admires the 'exquisite care' French jurisprudence is said to show in delimiting the scope of these two activities, in that the *Conseil d'Etat* limits itself to annulment and does not seek to fill the gap thus created by a positive direction as to what is to be done. This is an example of a legal nicety which is effectively a bludgeon; does not every *actuante* know that an administrative negation, an annulment or a mere failure to act, can resound every bit as loudly as the most positive and constructive decision?

Hamson illustrates the working of the *Conseil d'Etat statuant au contentieux* by reciting at some length the proceedings in a certain *affaire de l'Ecole Nationale*.[2] Certain young men presented themselves as candidates for a Civil Service competition. They were excluded from the list of candidates by the appropriate Minister who was acting under authority delegated to him by the Prime Minister. Each of the young men appealed to the *Conseil d'Etat* and there followed what was, in effect, a long 'public dialogue between the *Conseil d'Etat* itself and a Minister at its bar.'[3] The dialogue was, in accordance with the normal procedure, in writing, and the production of documents was demanded. The Minister at first tried to refuse to produce what was required, but he was ultimately obliged to do so. It is hardly too much to say that to Hamson this spectacle of a Minister publicly eating humble pie is little short of delicious, the more particularly, no doubt, because lawyers in England sometimes find themselves up against difficulties when the Crown claims privilege and declines to produce certain official documents. In the *affaire de l'Ecole Nationale* the Minister has ultimately to rescind his decision and the candidates are allowed to have their names restored to the list.

[1] Marques de las Marismas, *La Institución del Consejo de Estado en la Actualidad* (1952), p. 8.

[2] The case is to be found in the *Grands arrêts de la jurisprudence administrative* (Collection Sirey, 1956), p. 382 ff.

[3] Hamson, p. 30.

A Minister may well be wrong, and when he is it is in general well that he should be brought to admit his fault and to reverse his decision. What is of interest here is not the mere fact that the Minister's decision was in fact reversed or even the frivolity of the lawyer's pleasure at seeing him brought to this pass, but the criteria by which the Minister's actions are judged. The claim is that the administrator and his act are by the *Conseil d'Etat* brought to 'the test of reason', and the gravest charge against the Minister is that he 'failed to make known the grounds of his decisions'.[1] No doubt it is in general a good thing that a Minister should explain what he is up to; it is an important part of government, and not only in a democracy, to do so so far as is necessary for the actions of the government to be effective. But the 'test of reason' is by no means a self-evident one. Nor is it by any means self-evident that that other reason, which Hamson dislikes so much, the 'reason of state' is altogether nefarious. Certainly the courts in this country are right to watch critically to see that the Crown's right to withhold the production of documents is not used excessively. Certainly the highest vigilance is justified in maintaining the right of *habeas corpus*. But the proper functioning of the machine of state, which, and which alone, justifies the refusal to produce certain documents, is a long term interest of everyone in the country, and although Hamson apparently regards the late Regulation 18B with great horror and shares the scandalized feelings of his French interlocutor in this matter, people at large in this country and not merely the government almost certainly felt that, however repugnant arbitrary imprisonment might be, in a time of war its moderate use ought to be preferred to the risk of a treason which would endanger all. It is not altogether irrelevant to the substantial merits of the argument that France was defeated and we were not. Hamson, however, is not much concerned with the substance of affairs. Like a good lawyer he is a man of forms. Even the admission that the activity of the *Conseil d'Etat* has kept in being 'an obsolete and sometimes corrupt administrative machine'[2] does not damp his enthusiasm for it. It must, however, damp ours. We are concerned with how in practice an effective government machine should be run, and

---

[1] Hamson, p. 18.   [2] Hamson, p. 140.

a mere glance at the progress of pure reason is a poor consolation for the growing debility of the state. The progress of the *Conseil d'Etat*, in certain directions, has proceeded *pari passu* with the decline of the French state. One may imagine the chagrin of Napoleon, its founder, at the present scope and nature of the activities of the *Conseil d'Etat*. Hamson records how in 1822 in *l'affaire Lafitte*, the *Conseil d'Etat* refused, for reasons of state, to entertain a claim that was good in law. He adds that this '*théorie du mobile politique*' was rejected at the outset of the Third Republic and has never since been revived. '*La théorie des actes de gouvernement est fort simple*', he quotes with approval, '*il n'y en a pas.*'[1] And he might have added that there was no government either, the Third Republic having proved its incapacity to survive. One should at least entertain the possibility of a connection, of a nature less strong, no doubt, than direct cause and effect, between the developing theory of administrative law and the general strength or weakness of the state. The views of 1822 on the 'reason of state' did not preserve the régime of those days; the laws of survival are much more complicated than that. But it is hardly to be denied that a certain weakening of the conception of government has played a part in the troubles and disasters of the French state in recent years. Already in 1851 Rouget is saying: 'In days gone past the *Conseil d'Etat* probably did recognize a *pouvoir discrétionnaire* which was practically equivalent to an *acte de gouvernement*. But this is now merely of historical interest.' What has taken its place? The conclusion of *l'affaire de l'Ecole Nationale* was that a man holding a lawful political opinion could not be excluded from the Civil Service, 'the "could not" turning on a *principle—l'égalite de l'accès etc.*'[2] This principle is constitutional in France, going back beyond the preamble to the Constitution of 1946 to the Declaration of Rights of 1789. In view of that principle, the *Conseil d'Etat* could, no doubt, not have decided *l'affaire de l'Ecole Nationale* otherwise than it did, and it is clearly no business of an outsider to comment on that decision itself. Of more general interest, however, is the scope of the work of the *Conseil d'Etat* as exhibited by this case, and the spirit in which it operates.

[1] Hamson, p. 153.   [2] Hamson, p. 82.

Administrator and Law in France

As regards the latter, the high manner in which Hamson and others speak of the rôle of the *Conseil d'Etat* is very remarkable. Hamson speaks of the sovereign power of Parliament being 'recognized' rather as if that were a generous concession, and even Plantey, himself an *auditeur au Conseil d'Etat* speaks of Parliament and the *Conseil* in one breath as, so to speak, peers. There is, in this conception, the power of parliament and the power of reason represented by the *Conseil*; what is missing is any conception of government as such, and of its powers and responsibilities. The popular voice, supposed to be heard in the Chamber, is good, the voice of reason, for all true Frenchmen, is good, but the power of the government is an iniquity. No state can stand on such foundations. It is hardly too much to say that Hamson's view of the matter puts the *Conseil d'Etat* in the last resort, above the state. 'It is in no sense a rival or superior administration',[1] he says. But is it not? At least it is the conscience of the administration, which in this country is in the keeping of Parliament, and in a sense, of the Ministers themselves who have, however, to maintain a dialogue with Parliament as Hamson describes Ministers doing, in France, also with the *Conseil d'Etat*. The *Conseil d'Etat* is 'the incarnation of the republican and revolutionary spirit';[2] while governments come and go it has a continuity and a unity, 'the continuance of a temper of mind'. In a remarkable passage Hamson speaks of the working of the *Conseil* as a 'quaker's meeting'[3] and says that its corporate sense depends more on a 'state of mind than on any text or regulation'. Some such guiding spirit there must certainly be in a state; but is it certain that an administrative court is the proper repository of it?

The habit of legal thought represented by the attribution to the official of a status which gives him, as it were, an existence in his own right, dresses him with certain privileges and regards him as holding a little parcel of the authority of a notional thing called the state, is very much of a piece with the habit which is content to see a Minister brought to a shadowy 'test of reason' before the subtle experts of the Palais-Royal where we would have him answerable to the patience or impatience of the inexpert and commonsense Members in West-

[1] Hamson, p. 185.   [2] Hamson, p. 136.   [3] Hamson, p. 60.

minster. These things reflect profound constitutional attitudes. British government and British administration are in a sense merely things that go on here, whereas French government and administration, with their written constitutions and juristic refinements, aspire as it were to a theoretical status. It must not be thought that these differences date back merely to 1789, or are merely revolutionary habits of thought, as certain words of Hamson might seem to suggest, though undoubtedly the failure of institutions may lead people to seek a certain solace in theory. Justinian had a hand in the matter and his influence in modern Europe, like the secondary influence of Napoleon, was not confined to France.

CHAPTER V

Administrative Procedure as Law

Law is woven into the texture of many continental administrations in a way which is entirely strange to us in Britain. From one point of view, this may be regarded as an unimportant bit of methodology. In the French Civil Service the pay, leave and hours of officials are regulated by legal instruments; in Britain, the same matters have to be regulated, but the provisions find their way, not into legal instruments but into office codes. These codes are, in turn, largely founded on agreements between the Departments as employers on the one hand and representatives of the staff on the other. The contents of continental legal instruments may in some cases have been the subject of similar agreements, though it is doubtful whether the scope of discussions on such matters, or the habit of discussion and agreement, is anywhere so deeply ingrained as it is here. Even if the same intimacy of consultation preceded the formulation of the typical legal instrument on establishment matters as commonly precedes the formulation of the provisions of our codes, the choice of the final form is not without a far-reaching practical significance. No one with experience of the working of voluntary agreements in industry, on the one hand, and statutory regulation, on the other, would be disposed to doubt this. The agreement can be administered by the parties concerned flexibly and with regard to the circumstances of odd cases, while legal regulation imports a rigidity into any procedure it touches.

The dignity which legal clothing lends to the customs and rules of the public service gives much continental writing on this subject a faintly comic turn to the insular mind used to regarding most of such rules as things merely tiresome and necessary, and the customs as matters to be taken for granted. And there is a suspicion that, with this superfluous dignity, something more than mere vocabulary may come between the official and reality. Consider this statement from Spain about office hours: 'One of the duties of the official is attendance at the office, the discharge of his function for at least six hours a day. Another provision says the public offices must be open for eight hours a day. The latter does not fit in well with the former. . . .'[1] Eight hours of office opening and a six hour working day! The situation is full of possibilities for the ingenious establishments officer and still more for the trade union critic who, perhaps fortunately for those concerned, is in Spain not allowed to open his mouth on such subjects. But it would have to be solemnly enshrined in legal forms to be thought worth serious consideration at all. Otherwise, one might in a simple-minded way not try to explain it but merely put it right. Consider also the provision which requires certain physical standards in primary school teachers not merely for the efficient discharge of their duties, but for the avoidance of ridicule, *para evitar el ridículo.*[2] Such a provision might in fact represent anything from a practice discreet and sensible to one at once unnecessarily conservative or even quite inhuman. On the face of it it would seem better if people merely felt their way in such matters and there were no law to appeal to. The excessive use of the law produces a superstitious belief that there are *two* realities, one of the law and the other of the real world, and there is the risk that the latter may be regarded as the less important. Perhaps sometimes the world of law is created because the contemplation of the real world has become intolerable. That might well account for the Spanish *ley de Bases* of 19 October 1889, proclaiming (for such a law binds no one but the government) the rules of bureaucratic procedure; such as that 'any solicitation, communication or instance arriving in the office by post or by other means should be registered within twenty-four hours and the same day passed to the responsible official, who

---

[1] Sabino Alvarez-Gendin, *Manual de Derecho administrativo español* (1954), p. 443.
[2] Alvarez-Gendin, p. 415.

would acknowledge receipt to the Registry. In the following eight days . . . etc.'[1]

One can imagine that at the origin of such a law would be the bitter experience that the dispatch of business was not in fact so punctual. The direct means of achieving an improvement would be by an overhaul of the office and its workings. No other solution would suggest itself to the British mind, and if motive power from outside were needed, it would come from the harrying of Ministers by Members of Parliament. Yet to deal with the matter by legal means is perhaps not so odd as might at first appear. In the first place, laws are commonly passed because some change is desiderated in the world of fact; there is nothing unusual in that world having appeared intolerable. And if it is objected that a law which binds only the government is in a different category from one binding on citizens or subjects it might be pointed out that even laws of the latter kind are made up to limit of the government at least provisionally, and that a general motive for law is to let people know where they stand so that they are in a measure freed from the fear of merely arbitrary changes. The law can of course be revised, and the rule of law is a less stable conception than it is sometimes made to appear, but in general it is more difficult to change the law than to revise a Ministerial pronouncement and thus far the security given by the former is superior. The superior security of the legal instrument, in the case of a procedural matter such as that dealt with in the *Ley de Bases* in question, rests wholly, however, on the supposition of the inferior reliability of the Minister. The existence of such a law suggests a public doubt as to the latter's effectiveness. Even if its content is wholly laudable, therefore, it is in itself to be taken less as a sign of good government than as a sign of suspected bad government. There are, in fact, other reasons for keeping free of legal entanglements in a matter of this kind. If the obligation which a law places on the subject are clearly known there is everything to be said for the procedure adopted being left to be devised and if need be altered by those who are to run the organization concerned. This proposition might seem self-evident to anyone who had ever had to run even a tobacco shop.

[1] Alvarez-Gendin, p. 640.

Administrative Procedure as Law

The great French administrative lawyer, Hauriou, in 1927 classified Spain as being, with France herself, one of the few countries with what could properly be called a *régime administratif*.[1] Britain has notoriously been regarded as the classic country without such a régime, and though it is now sometimes doubted whether this classification is exact, significant differences between our way of doing things and that of the countries with an administrative régime undoubtedly remain. The political character of the Spanish régime is very different from that of the French, but Hauriou's lumping together of France and Spain as having administrations of a common type is not denied by contemporary Spanish authorities. Spain still looks towards France for the basis of her administrative law though deviations from the French pattern are apt to be strongly emphasized.[2] The Spanish administration is true to the type of *régime administratif* in exercising many powers which in this country are exercised by the courts. There has recently been some increase in the supervision of the administration by the ordinary courts,[3] but the administration can itself punish certain infractions by fines or, in default of payment, by imprisonment.

Provisions of this kind, so foreign to our conception of what the administration is or does, are not uncommon in other lands, and a notable example is to be found embodied in what is probably the most complete of all codes of administrative procedure, that of Austria. The Hapsburgs diffused over the eastern marches of Europe the regulating influence of a disciplined bureaucracy and since the disappearance of the Hapsburg régime, but true to its spirit, Austria has codified its administrative practice in a single comprehensive law, while Czechoslovakia, Yugoslavia and Poland have adopted similar systems.

[1] See *Revue internationale des Sciences administratives*, Vol. XXII, (1956), No. 2. This number is devoted to Spanish studies. Of particular interest is the article on *Les caractères spécifiques du droit administratif espagnol*, by Fernando Garrido Falla.

[2] Cf. *El Consejo de Estado Español y las influencias francesas a lo largo de su evolución*, by Luis Jordana de Pozas (1953).

[3] The transfer of business from an administrative tribunal to the ordinary courts is not necessarily a gain to those concerned. The abolition of the procedure known as *recurso de agravios*, under which state employees could appeal to the *consejo de estado* on any matter affecting their conditions of service, seems to have been planned with the object of reducing the number of such appeals, which were running at about 3,000 a year, to some much smaller number (perhaps about 200). Access to the ordinary courts is more difficult and more expensive.

Administrative Procedure as Law

The Austrian General Law of Administrative Procedure (*AVG* 1950)[1] is nothing less than the legal solution to all administrative problems. We of course possess many enactments, such as the National Service Acts, which lay down bits of procedure for special purposes, and so protect the citizen, it is hoped, against bureaucratic oppression in a particular field. The Austrians, however, are the happy discoverers of a system which is an insurance against *all* such oppression. A General Law indeed!

First come some general provisions. The competence of an authority to deal with a particular subject-matter, or to deal with it in a particular area, will normally be found to have been defined in particular laws. The General Law, leaving nothing to chance, provides no less than three tiers of authorities for cases as to which the law is silent. The law in Austria is rarely silent on the subject of appropriate authorities, but where it is, the general local and regional administrative authorities, and finally the Ministry of the Interior, take the matter upon their already weighted shoulders. Each authority—mercifully, one may think—is regarded as an entity, so that although you may pursue your dossier from A to B and so to C, you are not entitled to inquire which of the seven men composing, say, authority A, is making trouble for you. The law already at this stage has about it a look of Kafka, who might well in 'The Trial' and 'The Castle' cast his melancholy into an administrative framework, for was he not employed as a minor official in Prague, operating laws which preceded the enlightenment of *AVG* 1950? You will know, or if you do not feel satisfied on the point you may challenge it, that if one of the seven men is your cousin *he* will not be allowed to deal with the case, for there is a provision that no official who is-interested in the matter in hand in such a way as to bring his impartiality in question, shall be entrusted with it. It is a comfort that, so to speak, that chap's signature will not be on your death warrant, though exactly what went on within authority A, where he is employed, you will not as you expire know. The authorities may summon people to appear before them. The summons has to set out where and when the business is to be done, in which capacity the person summoned is to appear, whether he has to

[1] *Allgemeines Verwaltungsverfahrensgesetz—AVG.* 1950, *Bundesgesetzblatt für die Republik Österreich*, 31st August 1950.

come personally or can send a representative, and what will happen if he does not come. A person so summoned has no choice but to turn up, and he can be forced to do so, though the authority can impose penalties only if they have given due notice in the summons that they will do so. Anyone in the public service whose presence is required by an authority is likely to find that his superior officer has been informed about the matter,[1] a provision which British Civil Servants would certainly regard as intrusive.

The whole thing is to be conceived as a kind of administrative snakes and ladders. A commentator, Dr. Mannlicher, explains that under this law anyone who has to deal with the authorities is 'no longer' (and the words suggests the tradition behind the law) 'the object of the authorities' activity, so that they can follow more or less whatever procedure seems good to them. He has rather—in accordance with the nature of the constitutional state[2]—become a participant in the procedure, which must follow certain rules.'[3] But the translation is too anodyne. Dr. Mannlicher speaks of the procedure '*dass sich nach bestimmten Regeln abzuspielen hat*'—which must be played out in accordance with certain rules. And it is impossible to read the General Law without feeling a keen sense for the game. A procedural flaw can ruin your opponent's chances. So, for example, an authority which is not proceeding according to all the rules can suddenly find itself, so to speak, back in square one. A legal representative can be employed to play the game for you, which may be expensive but will presumably improve your chances of victory, or, if you are going to lose, of delay. The rights are not, however, all on the side of the gentleman who used to be called the subject but is now said to have become a collaborator in the game. If you can employ a lawyer to outwit the authorities or can try your own hand at outwitting them, so can the authorities, no doubt not unskilled in the matter, try to outwit you. If you have been guilty of a procedural flaw you too may be back in square one. If you are a simple soul and have

---

[1] *AVG* 1950, Section 20.

[2] This dictionary translation of *Rechtsstaat* does not do justice to the legal emphasis of the German word.

[3] Egbert Mannlicher. *Das Verwalfungsverfahren*, 6th edition (Vienna), 1953.

to rely on wits more accustomed to housework or to milking cows than to playing legal games in accordance with elaborate rules you may find all this a little confusing. What you will understand, however, is that the authorities, besides being good at the game, have another card up their sleeves. This joker is not one permitted to the emancipated participant. The authorities can fine or imprison you if you become too tiresome to them. Perhaps on so grave a matter a quotation from the law would be better than what may look like a frivolous summary. The terms of the section are that 'persons who disturb the official proceedings or offend against propriety by unseemly conduct are to be admonished; and if the admonishment does no good they can after due warning be silenced and removed and told to find a proxy to take their place, or punished by a fine up to 200 schillings or three days imprisonment.'[1] One can see the awkward customer being suppressed like the lizard in 'Alice'. Or again: 'Against persons who manifestly and wilfully impede the activity of the authority or, with a view to protracting the affair make false statements, the authority can impose a penalty for wilfulness (*Mutwillenstrafe*) up to 500 schillings and, in case of default, up to three days imprisonment.'[2] An even more pleasing provision is that similar penalties can be imposed on 'persons who in written statements employ an insulting manner.'[3] As to the carrying out of the penalty, if the authority simply have not room to keep you in custody themselves they can hand you over to the local jail. It is a consolation to know that, while you are doing time at the pleasure of the administrative authority you may wear your own clothes and even, if you are willing to pay for it, order your favourite Wurst. All that is provided for in the Administrative Penalties Law (*VStG* 1950)[4] which also makes it clear that if you don't of your own volition find something to do in prison (you should have brought your knitting with you!) the authority will find some little task suitable to your capacities and knowledge, but they won't put you to outdoor work unless you agree to it.

[1] *AVG* 1950, Section 34 (2)   [2] *AVG* 1950, Section 35.
[3] *AVG* 1950, Section 34 (3).
[4] *Verwaltungsstrafgesetz*, *VStG* 1950; *Bundesgesetzblatt für die Republik Österreich*, 31st August 1950.

This thing does not, to someone accustomed to the British system, look at all reassuring. Yet the General Law of Administrative Procedure has considerable merits, and even the Penalties Law might well be welcome if one had been used to worse. The latter is indeed mild and humane; it is less the penalties, than the manner in which they are imposed, which seem odd to the simple islander. The administrative authorities themselves impose them, as we have seen; and in this context that broad expression means the electricity authority or the water company as well as the police and the officials who with us would be Civil Servants. The Federal Chancellery, it is true, dislikes the imposition of penalties by the merely specialized authorities and would like to see all powers of this kind concentrated in the general authorities, as most of them in fact are already; but it is some way off achieving this objective. The authorities impose their penalties without any previous control by the courts; it is only afterwards that you can object, and your right to do so may be either in the ordinary or in the administrative court. At least as a citizen you have the advantage of knowing exactly the extent of your liability or punishment. By the authorities the law is thought of as safeguarding the objects of the authority concerned and as taking trivial cases away from the courts. There might be other advantages. But one cannot even imagine a dreamy look coming into the eyes of the British official at the thought of possessing such a weapon; on the contrary he could never sleep with the thing under his pillow.

The Law of Administrative Procedure, for all the oddity of its conception—from our point of view—is in its form a piece of considerable elegance. Moreover, it contains many provisions which are merely a statement of good administrative practice which with us would not be considered to need legal sanction. For example, a written note has, in appropriate cases, to be taken of oral statements, and the notes are to be so prepared that, 'leaving out all irrelevancies', the course and substance of the conversation are recorded. In general, parties are to have the sight of documents they need to be acquainted with in order to make good their rights; but this permission is not given without weighty precautions and reservations on the part of the authorities.[1] Oral hearings are to be such that every party must be given an opportunity to bring forward any relevant views. The present law is a revision of that originally introduced in 1925, in the Republic's period of consolidation after the end of the Empire. It was not invented out of nothing. It was, in substance, a codification—a brilliant one—of the work of the Administrative Court over the previous years of its existence (the Court was established in 1876). It is, in fact only in relation to the work of the Administrative Court that the law on procedure is to be understood. What that law in fact does is to prescribe the steps which have to be taken before a matter can properly come before the court. It is not its function to hear cases until all the procedures defined to the Law of Administrative Procedure have been exhausted. Looked at from the point of view of the court, the function of the Law may be said to be to define when a decision has been taken against which an appeal could lie to the Court. What, in the sense of this law, is a decision? In the mass of correspondence which emanates from Austrian authorities as from ours, how is one to know when one has got something that one can appeal against? The theoretical answer is easy. Every decision is to be expressly so labelled.[2] In practice it may not be, through the failure of the authority issuing it to address itself to this point, and indeed not only the recipient but the authority may not in practice be clear that a decision has been issued. The mere labelling is of course not enough. The law prescribes certain other requirements. If the decision is one that is not necessarily agreeable to all concerned, it has to include a statement of the facts on which it is based and an indication of the legal powers under which it is made. It should have been taken after a whole rigmarole of procedures relating to the ascertaining of the facts has been carried out. A well-trained servant of the state will, no doubt, arrive and set out the decision in any important matter more or less in the manner prescribed. A mere failure to comply with the forms is not, however, in practice regarded as nullifying the decision, so that although the law is potentially a game of snakes and ladders, in practice it may not be so elaborately played. The law govern-

[1] *AVG* 1950, Section 17 (2).
[2] *AVG* 1950, Section 58.

68

ing the practice of the administrative court[1] directs that a decision is to be considered as null and void on procedural grounds only if, by strictly following the procedure, the authority concerned could have come to a decision different from the one it did in fact reach. This amounts to saying that the law is a statement of what should be done rather than of what must be done. The administrative court has, in fact, regarded as a decision any document emanating from a competent authority which either imposes a duty or gives a right.

One may well wonder why, in the face of so much common sense on the part of the court, it is necessary to have a procedural law at all. The historical answer would be, no doubt, that people accustomed to a somewhat high-handed bureaucracy felt the need for some re-assurance, and that while administrative officials could not be tied down to so rigid a procedure as the courts there could be a declaration that they would conduct themselves in a manner which would give the citizen of the new republic every chance of getting his rights. People naturally talk a lot about their rights in a period of insecurity following a revolutionary change, and it is hardly too much to say that the post-Napoleonic legal system of Europe as a whole is a product of such insecurity. The Austrians, in giving legal form, by a considerable exercise of ingenuity, to their declaration as to the good behaviour of republican officials, were only going a step further on well-trodden paths. Once there, and in spite of the powers of the administrative court to disregard inessential deviations from it, the law no doubt does contribute towards a certain standard of official behaviour.[2] The authority that has ignored the spirit of the law will not look well in court, and in Austria, if a few older officials are still inclined to more high-handed ways, generations by whom the spirit of the new law is accepted have since grown up. In a population of administrator-jurists a change in outlook could hardly be brought about in any other way than through the use of a legal instrument. Even so, this method, though perhaps the best in the circumstances, need not excite the envy of a country

---

[1] *Verwaltungsgerichtshofgesetz*, Section 42.

[2] It might well be argued that a similar law might be extremely valuable in encouraging a more civilized conduct in, say, Russian administrators.

whose administration, like ours, enjoys a more supple and subtle form of control. The control with us is that provided by public opinion and particularly public opinion as expressed through Members of Parliament. That exercised by the courts, though not negligible, is comparatively occasional and is generally less searching. It would not be a gain to exchange an administration sensitive to the rough tests of common sense and public opinion for one obsessed with anxiety about procedural points and the sort of figure it would cut before the judges of an administrative court.

CHAPTER VI

The Judge and the Administrator

The classic British criticism of continental systems of administrative law has been that by its association with administration the law loses its independence, that it is, so to speak, perverted by proximity to the seat of power. Once the British lawyer is satisfied, as Hamson was in the case of the *Conseil d'Etat*, of the effective independence of an administrative tribunal, his distrust may turn, as Hamson's did, to admiration. The adminstrator's point of view is different. He is concerned—and it is surely a legitimate professional concern—at the damage which may be done to the administration by the inept intrusion of the law. The slowness of legal procedures, and the stiffness which excessive prescription may introduce into the practical business of government, are what most interest him. What repels him in the continental systems is a certain Byzantinism. French law as contrasted with English law, French administration as contrasted with British administration or, for that matter, the Roman Church as contrasted with the English Church, have characteristics which are observable in Justinian's code. 'A preference for abstract standards, referable to definite and conscious ethical conceptions, . . . and a taste for logical arrangement which sometimes degenerates into the multiplication of unreal and practically useless distinctions.'[1] The application of the words H. F. Jolowicz uses to describe the *Corpus Juris* is clear. We may not unreasonably think ourselves nearer 'the practical spirit of the true Roman law', to which 'the subsequent development of generalizations and classifications' was 'alien'.[2] Justin-

[1] H. F. Jolowicz, *Historical Introduction to the Study of Roman Law*, second edition (1952), p. 529.
[2] Jolowicz, p. 522.

71

ian's cap fits exactly the French laws on the status of the *fonctionnaire* or the Austrian Law of Administrative Procedure as showing 'a taste for excessive regulation by statute of matters to which fixed rules can hardly, by their very nature, be applied with success'.[1]

It may be said that the British administrator on the whole avoids law-making when he can, though it may be thought, from the look of the bulging statute-book, that his efforts have been singularly unsuccessful. The extent to which legislation can be avoided is strictly limited, because a Minister who is to embark on any new line of action is likely to need parliamentary authority to do so. But, although there have been exceptions, the administrator's general practice, in this country, has been to shun legislation where other means can achieve his ends. He prefers to see things taking shape in the real world before he invents an elaborate legal construction, because he knows that with such a construction, devised *in vacuo*, nothing may ever correspond. In an obscure way, he is not unfriendly to the old conception of law as custom, and where the subject-matter of the business allows he may try to stimulate a habit of behaviour and recommend legislation only when the habit is widely enough diffused to bring effective enforcement reasonably within sight. Where the nature of the business does not allow of such a proceeding he likes, by consultation with the parties most immediately affected, to ensure the viability of what is to be proposed. This conservative and realistic habit of mind is very different from that found in a number of countries where the traditions of the lawyer-administrator prevail. In France the administrator's thoughts run very early to a draft law, embodying an ideal conceived *in vacuo*, the execution of which, in the form proposed, may prove impracticable. A similar habit of mind accounts for the edifying nature of the reading matter which is to be found on the statute-books of many primitive or ill-governed countries.

The British administrator, in short, likes to see the law growing out of practice and crowning it, but he is far from any prejudice against the state taking a proper initiative. Indeed, the only distinction that interests him is that between the

[1] Jolowicz, p. 521.

practicable and the impracticable, and a flood of legislation which gives Ministers new powers is unsatisfactory only if he feels that it is coming at a pace which puts in doubt the effectiveness of the execution. This practical concern may be due in part to tradition and to the national habit of mind. It is also due to the fact that, under our system, the administrator who plans the content of the legislation on a particular topic is normally also the man who, even though the government should change, will be responsible for seeing that the machinery it sets up works properly, and for drafting the briefs, letters and replies to parliamentary questions in which the Minister of the day will be forced to demonstrate the effectiveness of his administration. The *politics* of a measure, in the sense in which parties use that term, genuinely do not exist for the British administrator, but the practicality of the thing is something of which he has daily cause to be even agonizingly aware. An amending bill which follows, after some years of working experience, a piece of established and accepted legislation, is likely to be the fruit of practical experience of administration and will be presented by the administrator to his political chief of the day in the knowledge that so far as the pure practicality of the thing can be demonstrated it is likely to be welcome to a British government of either political colour. To the making of the estimate of practicality there goes, of course, an estimate of the reactions of the special publics concerned or of the general public. That is the concern of both politician and administrator. The mechanical practicality of the thing is not likely to be in question where the legislation has grown out of practice.

The British administrator who has cast a look in the direction of continental systems of administration will moreover become aware that the lawyers brought up in the empirical muddling of the common law are nearer his own way of thinking than are his fellow-administrators on the continent, brought up under entirely different legal systems. His attitude none the less differs in important respects from that of the British lawyer. The lawyer in England, unlike his colleagues in the Roman law countries, has behind him a professional history which tends to separate him from the administrator. He is not accustomed to think of justice, as they do in France, as a 'government service like the provision of education or roads'.[1] He is conscious of belonging to a kind of independent corporation, knowing that 'Parliament only passes statutes affecting the organization of the courts on the advice or suggestion of the legal profession'.[2] He is haunted by the ghost of Sir Edward Coke, and is inclined to believe in the common law as in a power independent of the state, forgetting that in so far as Parliamentary supremacy was established in 1688 the standing of the common law fell with that of the royal prerogative. The administrator thinks of the law as an instrument for getting things done. His legal outlook is formed entirely by the conception of statute law, and it may be said that on this account his view of the law is at once more up-to-date and, in certain reaches, shallower than that of the lawyer. Above all, and as compared both with the British lawyer and the foreign administrator, he regards law as secondary, and in this he is at once modern and affiliated to traditions of government which are anything but modern.

In recent times administrators in this country have been the object of severe criticism, one might say of violent attack, from the lawyers. Hamson's book may be regarded as a by-product of this hostile movement. The most famous protagonist in the lawyer's quarrel was the late Lord Hewart. *The New Despotism* was written—to use a phrase Hewart quotes from North's Plutarch—to pull down the pride and stomach of the clerks. The lives of Cato and the late Lord Chief Justice of England were not quite parallel. The former was more like an energetic Minister raising hell in his department; he 'made great alteration amongst the clerks and officers of the Treasury.'[3] The latter was not convinced that Ministers could have such power, and he was concerned to abate the power of the executive lest the liberty of the subject and the standing of the judiciary should themselves be abated. To this task Hewart brought a partiality not altogether judicial, and only a moderate respect for the High Court of Parliament. In his anxiety to save the House of Commons from

[1] G.R.Y. Radcliffe and Geoffrey Cross, *The English Legal System*, third edition, p. 393.

[2] Radcliffe and Cross, p. 393.

[3] Lord Hewart, *The New Despotism* (1929), p. 160.

The Judge and the Administrator

the officials he did not scruple to suggest that it did not know what it was about when it delegated to Ministers power to make certain statutory orders and that it was the helpless victim of a plot 'intended to produce, and in practice producing, a despotic power'.[1] The Lord Chief Justice was not called to the Bar of the House and made to purge his contempt, but he might have been. The new despotism 'gives Parliament an anaesthetic'. Its strategy is 'to render the will, or the caprice, of the Executive unfettered and supreme'.[2] The language is not moderate.

The evidence for this plot Hewart found in enactments passed by Parliament itself. Parliament was 'being outmanœuvred'[3] by being persuaded, apparently by officials, to pass such legislation as that Rating and Valuation Act (1925) of which Section 67 was entitled—'pleasantly enough' as Hewart says—'Power to remove difficulties'. The fact that the public departments were in the charge of Ministers, and that Parliament, having specified with some precision how the rating and valuation system was to work, chose to leave some of the details to them, was indifferent to Hewart. He evidently did not believe that Ministers had the energy of Cato, or that they would 'thoroughly understand what the clerks and registers should be'. He was one of those who, in the words of Mr. Justice Eve which he quotes, 'were convinced that the best Government was that which governed least'.[4] Many people, and certainly many Civil Servants among them, have the same sentiments. But 'less government' is not what Parliament has judged fit for the times and assuredly since 1929 the electorate have not wanted to be saved, even by judges, from officials with power to run effectively a socialized state. What they have wanted is parliamentary control of the direction of government, and of the measures introduced, and the power to protest, through their Member of Parliament, if they thought the laws were ineptly administered. Mr. Justice Eve's remark, however true in some contexts, is in the context of an England where the main policies are popularly determined, simply not true at all. It is no more good government to govern a socialized democracy with two proctors and a policeman than it would have been to govern

[1] Hewart, p. 14. [2] Hewart, p. 17. [3] Hewart, p. 16. [4] Hewart, p. 161.

75

The Judge and the Administrator

pre-industrial England with a Civil Service of the size we have now. Hewart's thesis, like Eve's, is based on a preference for the common-law world where the upper class and a prosperous middle class gave work to lawyers by much litigation *inter se*. It is amusing to see that Hewart is inclined to forgive the lawyers in the government service. 'The Law Officers of the Crown, the Treasury solicitor, and the Parliamentary draftsmen have from time to time used all their influence to prevent, or mitigate, acts which they could not approve.'[1] Parliament is blamed for not seeing things with a lawyer's eyes, and the non-legal officials, the real villains, are contrasted unfavourably with the legal gentlemen employed by the State. The very notion which Hewart attaches to the idea of 'responsibility' is one which belongs to a world of substantial burgesses the passing of which one may well, from certain points of view, regret. The official is anonymous and removable; he will do anything for pay. His answerability to his superiors, to his Minister—on which after all much, even from the basest point of view, depends—and his Minister's answerability to Parliament on which, in turn, much of the Minister's reputation and future depends, do not constitute 'responsibility' for Lord Hewart. His notion, and it is well grounded—it is indeed, basically the notion of responsibility before God—is that the judge, unlike these others, is responsible precisely because he is answerable to no man. He gives reasons for his decision, which are taken after public argument, and whether or not his decision is liked he can scarcely be called to account for it accept by a superior court, unless it be by the improbable and extreme remedy of a petition by both Houses of Parliament. In the popular view, it is the difficulty that there in fact is in removing the ordinary official which may tempt him to irresponsibility because people have a parliamentary notion of responsibility and think that responsibility means, in some form, responsibility to them. Hewart is in fact turning his back on this and saying that judges are responsible in much the same way as was Charles I, who did not regard himself as responsible to the people. One is entitled to think that Hewart was not altogether wrong in his conception and that the democratic notion of responsibility

[1] Hewart, p. 22.

76

The Judge and the Administrator

needs, in a sane constitution, to be supplemented by some other, different in kind. But the idea is not one for which, in the present way of the policy, much popularity is to be expected.

Hewart was the defender of 'a polity wherein the people make their laws, and independent judges administer them',[1] but although he imagined that in so doing he was defending the present liberties of the subject he was in fact looking back, for that polity is the same in which most of the administration of the country was in the hands of magistrates. The respective territories of administrative and judicial activity are by no means clearly defined. W. A. Robson, who could hardly be suspected of partiality for the official's side of the quarrel, has spoken clearly on this matter. 'It is very difficult to discover any adequate method by which, in a highly developed country like England, judicial functions can be clearly distinguished from administrative functions. Mere names are of no avail, for . . . judges often administer and administrators often judge.'[2] And Maitland, in reference to Montesquieu's assertion (*Esprit des Lois* XI, ci) about the separation in this country of administration and judicature, comments that 'in England, of all places in the world . . . the two have for ages been inextricably blended.'[3] Decisions, such as whether the child should be brought up as a Papist, or about the suitability of a marriage, which may arise in connection with a ward of court, are essentially administrative decisions. They are questions of what in the circumstances, and within the law, is the sensible thing to be done. These are decisions taken by judges. On the other hand, the official has often to determine questions of right, and to administer the law is, inevitably, to interpet it. The question of the distinction between a judicial and an administrative act often comes before the courts, because 'orders of prohibition and *certiorari* will lie only in respect of judicial acts, and not for those of an administrative or ministerial character', but Robson concludes that the decided cases 'disclose no coherent principle' and merely demonstrate, 'by the very confusion of thought they present, the difficulty of arriving at a clear basis of distinction.'[4] Formerly it was con-

[1] Hewart, p. 16.
[2] W. A. Robson, *Justice and Administrative Law*, third edition (1951), p. 4.
[3] F. M. Maitland, *Collected Papers*, Vol. I, p. 478, quoted in Robson, op. cit.
[4] Robson, p. 5.

venient to give a number of administrative functions to justices of the peace, which in a loose and rudimentary administrative system was well enough. But for the last century or more the government has, in general, had to look elsewhere for the machinery of administration. Although it is obviously of the utmost public importance that certain matters should be dealt with in an open court, and the foundation of our liberties would be irrevocably weakened if they were not, yet in respect of some matters it may be said that it is largely a matter of historical accident whether they are dealt with by the judiciary or the executive. As Robson puts it, 'plenty of administrative acts are performed by judges arrayed in scarlet and ermine and surrounded by all the pomp and circumstance which for centuries has attended the administration of justice by the King's judges. And many an obscure Civil Servant, sitting bespectacled in a quiet office, is engaged in activities which partake of a judicial character.'[1]

The lesser pomp is not necessarily undesirable. Provided that the public can make trouble if things go wrong, as in fact, through their Member of Parliament, they can, there is something to be said for going to discuss something with men in an office rather than submitting to all the formalities of a court. It will probably take you less time; it will almost certainly be cheaper to your and to the public purse. The price of ermine and scarlet, and even of wigs and black gowns, is high, and Hewart shows some sensitivity on this point. Moreover, it is the nature of much of the business to be decided that it involves a detailed knowledge of a great organization and of a particular subject-matter, which the courts will not take tacitly.

The relationship between judicial and administrative proceedings is dealt with at some length in Roscoe Pound's *Administrative Law: Its Growth, Procedure and Significance*.[2] The first of these lectures is entitled 'The Place of Administration in the Legal Order'. That is a legitimate and useful subject of inquiry. No less useful, and surely no less legitimate even if less acceptable to the legal mind, would be a study of the place of the legal

[1] Robson, p. 27.
[2] Roscoe Pound, *Administrative Law: its Growth, Procedure and Significance* (Pittsburgh, 1942).

order in administration. If in classical and medieval theory administration holds a subordinate place and is, as it were, a mere dependency of *suprema lex*, it is a matter of fact that only in a society with administration enough to hold it together can there be any question at all of a lawyer's law. And even in our own time we have seen that the failure of government which permits the irruption of hostile forces into a territory may, if the invader be a barbarian, result in the failure of the law. The law, in any refined sense, is in fact protected as the consciences of those who refuse to fight are protected by those who do.

The exercise of justice is, indeed, a part of the attributions of the supreme authority which only a fortunate history has taught us to regard as separable. From this separation has sprung a liberty which we are right to guard jealously, but if the means we choose to defend it were to result in the destruction of the administration we should, in fact, be going about to destroy justice itself. It is one of the merits of Roscoe Pound's book that he is aware of the close link between justice and administration. He is very much on the lawyer's side of the quarrel that must always go on between these two, but he realizes that there is a price to be paid for the liberty that he defends. 'We must pay a certain price for freedom; and a reasonable balance between efficiency and individual rights is that price.'[1] In any particular historical situation, it has to be decided how much efficiency can be afforded in return for the goods of justice. Roscoe Pound was giving his lectures in the autumn of 1940, in the security of Pittsburgh. On this side of the Atlantic the price of the full measure of our freedom had become a bit high, and we had Regulation 18B as in the last resort any nation which has the will to live will fall back on the Roman formula: *Salus reipublicae suprema lex esto*! The area of judicial justice changes with the times, and what is lost or gained by the courts may be gained or lost by administration. For not only do these two methods or institutions depend from the same source; they are different forms of the same activity. To hold that they are the same by no means necessarily implies acceptance of the Marxist view in which, as Pound says, 'there

[1] Pound, p. 56.

is no room for law'. It may instead imply the view that all government should be subject to a law which is anterior to the state's and to which those who govern as well as those who judge are answerable. In any case, the identity of the two activities may be studied without reference to any justificatory theory. 'To this day, in the Roman-law world, the judiciary are thought of as a part of the administrative hierarchy.'[1] It is we and the Americans who are odd. It is interesting to see how far the descriptions Roscoe Pound gives of judicial activity are, in fact, equally applicable to a competent administration. 'Judicial interpretation postulates that a formula prescribed by statute was meant to cover certain definite areas of fact discoverable and to be discovered.'[2] The judge has to decide how the particular case falls within those areas. But that is precisely the work of the administrator in so far as the latter is concerned with determining or adjudicating. In most cases the answer is so plain for all to see that there is no question of recourse to the courts. In a few difficult cases a more elaborate and expensive procedure is thought to be justified, and because of the doubt as to the outcome it is felt that all the steps by which a solution is reached should be public and so open to criticism. Roscoe Pound's description of administrative action is much coloured by the peculiarities of the American system. The lay administrators, he says, in contradistinction to the man of law 'are prone to act, in deciding, as very likely they properly may in directing, as if every case were unique'.[3] This surely reflects the outlook of the business man turned official. Nothing could be less like the procedures of the wary professional bureaucrat, for whom precedent is so important and whom the anxiety to secure uniformity is always gnawing. The defence of 'administrative determinations' which Pound quotes in order to destroy is likewise one which would not have occurred to an official in this country. One of the points of the defence is that the process of administrative determination 'as distinguished from the judicial process, moves in a narrow field' so that 'the administrative is not open to the broad range of human sympathies to which the judicial process is subject.'[4] This extraordinary defence, the validity of which Pound rightly calls in question,

---

[1] Pound, p. 94.   [2] Pound, p. 99.   [3] Pound, p. 62.   [4] Pound, p. 63.

would be as repugnant to a British Civil Servant as to the American lawyer. Similarly as to the second point of the defence of administrative determinations, 'that singleness of concern quickly develops a professionalism of spirit—an attitude which perhaps more than rules affords assurance of informed and balanced judgments'.[1] The British Civil Servant would be less likely to see himself in that than in Roscoe Pound's reply which sets out what are said to be the advantages of the lawyer's outlook: 'But does the professionalism which grows from preoccupation with a single type of controversy afford the check that is to be found in long continued occupation with controversies of every type?'[2] That, certainly, as well describes the type of general administrator which the British system seeks to produce as it does the lawyer or the judge. The guarantee of impartiality which Pound sees in the permanence of judges as contrasted with the doubtful tenure of 'boards' is also one which has more force on his side of the Atlantic than on ours.

The respective areas of administration and the judicial process are not something to be determined *a priori*. They are matters to be determined by the joint light of tradition and the needs of the time, the object being always to maintain that 'balance between general security and the individual life'[3] of which Pound speaks. More generally, one may say that if the continental conception of the lawyer-administrator involves too close an identification between legal and administrative processes, an attack such as Hewart's involves much too sharp a view of the singularity of the legal process. But if there is a similarity, in certain respects, between what the judge does and what the administrator does, there is also a difference in their points of view. A judge's own sense of what is good for the country may well enter into certain of his judgments, for example in the matter of obscenity. The administrator, on the other hand, has as his main and ultimate concern, what is good in terms constitutionally appropriate: what will keep his Minister going. He looks at the thing from the point of view of Ministerial responsibility, a matter which lies at the root of our liberties but of which neither Hamson nor Hewart shows much understanding. The judge has his sense of continuity; the

[1] Pound, p. 63.   [2] Pound, p. 63.   [3] Pound, p. 88.

administrator has his, not less acute but different, looking towards the future more than towards the past, and concerned with the persistence of the Queen's government, as such and without regard to its political complexion, and more remotely with the continuance of the realm itself.

CHAPTER VII

The Administrator as Governor

If a concern for the coherence and continuance of government is implicit in what the British administrator does, it is a characteristic of the British system that no official is explicitly charged with these matters. In many European countries things are different. There are, in addition to the numerous officials who, like their British counterparts, have their particular charges, a small number of trusted men who, in some sense, act as the general overseers of the country. The central government feels the need, as ours does not, of having at key points throughout the country men whose function is to act as their general agents and representatives. These men are, in some sort, provincial governors.

In Spain the officials who answer to this description go frankly by the name of *Gobernadores civiles*. A Spanish writer on administrative law lists a number of more or less remote precedents of this office showing, as he says, 'that the central power has always needed its representatives in the various regions of the country'.[1] The praetors of Roman times were the first of a long succession known at various times as *corregidores asistentes, intendentes, jefes politicos*. The *Gobernadores civiles* have the general duty of carrying out the laws and policies of the government; they have responsibility for public order, with all that this can imply; and they are the heads of the central administration in the province they govern. They provide a link—to put it no more strongly—between the central government and the local authorities, for they act as heads of the local administration and have a general oversight over those authorities. In Italy each province has its *prefetto*

[1] Alvarez-Gendin, p. 55 ff.

'the highest authority of the state in the province, representing the government in its unity . . . the only local authority recognized as having a certain power of a political nature.'[1] The general attributions of the *prefetto* are not dissimilar from those of the *gobernador civil.*

The official of this general type who is most familiar to people in this country is the French *préfet*, who, owing to the influence of Napoleon and the prestige of the French service, is in some sense the model for Europe at large. It is not the custom among French writers on administrative law to boast of the ancestry of the *préfet* as Alvarez-Gendin does of that of the *Gobernador civil*. It would not be in accordance with the revolutionary mythology which hangs about north of the Pyrenees. None the less, it is generally recognized that in establishing his hundred overseers, to whom he gave, as a First Consul understandably might, a name formerly given to Roman provincial governors, Napoleon was in a manner resuscitating the system of *intendants* which had prevailed under the *ancien régime*. There had been thirty-six *intendants*, each managing the business of a province as the direct agent of Paris,[2] and just as the British traveller nowadays will find in the *préfet* a governing official of a type unknown in this country, so the eighteenth-century traveller must have remembered, as he extolled the superior liberties he enjoyed at home, that in his county the central power was represented by nothing more permanent or arbitrary than the judges or circuit, unless it were by the Lord Lieutenant or by himself and his friends holding commissions as justices of the peace. Like other offices and institutions created by Napoleon, that of *préfet* has undergone significant changes in the last hundred and fifty years, but the *préfet* remains, like the *intendant* before him, solidly and unmistakably the central personage of his district, and he holds that position as being, explicitly, the direct agent and general representative of the central government. He can be sacked by the government at any moment, though the cadre of *préfets* is in fact considerably more stable than is suggested by this rule of formal dependency.

It would be hard to imagine an official with a more compre-

[1] Aldo M. Sandulli, *Manuale di Diritto Amministrativo*, p. 181.
[2] Alexis de Tocqueville, *L'Ancien Régime et la Révolution*, passim.

hensive load of attributions than those which rest upon the *préfet*. He is '*dépositaire dans le département de l'autorité de l'Etat*',[1] and he is the chief representative of all the Ministers. He supervises the execution of laws, orders and government decisions. He represents the national interests in general and as the chief Civil Servant of the department in theory directs the activities of all the others. He keeps an eye on various local government activities, acting as a sort of permanent secretary to the elected *conseil général* of the *département* and having, besides, the power to suspend and replace mayors and to approve or to withhold approval of certain deliberations of municipal councils. No British official has anything like this range of duties; above all, none has this kind of responsibility. In case of a break-down of public order, Frenchmen would be likely to turn to their *préfet*, if they turned to anyone, for a lead. In Britain people in trouble do come in great numbers to seek the help of the officials of the several ministries, but if any kind of public lead were required they would expect to find it elsewhere, even though the figure-head provided in fact contributed little that did not come out of the official advices he received. It was on this principle that the government, during the war, took the precaution of appointing Regional Commissioners who could have taken over the administration of their areas in case of a breakdown. It would never have done to suggest that free-born Englishmen should submit themselves to the judgment of a Civil Servant. The Regional Commissioners, whose effectiveness as co-ordinators and directors was happily never fully tested, and who stood much further out of the ordinary cadre of officials than do the prefects, were the nearest approximation we have known to the French officials who do, effectively, and in spite of the misgivings that one cannot but entertain on a close acquaintance with the system, form the backbone, in a sense the whole skeleton, of French outstationed administration.

The British administrator, and indeed the British Civil Servant in general, tries to be as far as possible invisible. The *préfet* is professionally prominent. Not only has he a sort of admiral's uniform which he puts on when he unveils a memorial

[1] Rolland, p. 181.

or takes the salute at a march past of the local garrison; he enjoys a certain modest luxury. He lives in the prefecture, and he and his lady hold a little provincial court, in which gather from time to time the leading members of the *conseil général* and other local notables. Among British Civil Servants, one would have to go to the Foreign Service, which is remote in spirit and function from the Home Civil Service, to encounter officials who made it their business to glitter in any but the dimmest way. None the less, the British administrator may feel himself in some respects more at home in a prefecture than with certain of the legal contortionists in Paris. While he cannot but be impressed by the skill and learning of the *Conseil d'Etat*, the outlook of the *préfet* is certainly nearer his own. The *préfet*, like the British administrator, is trying, with the help of or in spite of the law, to get something done. Moreover, the range of business which passes before him is wide—wider, indeed, than that which falls in the way of the British administrator— and he has therefore something of the amateurishness which is a professional requirement in Whitehall, a knack of picking up any business, whatever it may be, and turning it into the way of government. But the British administrator's trimming of the business to fit the requirements of government is of course the trimming that is required for preparing it or dispatching it on behalf of a single Minister on whose doorstep he lives and to whom he is responsible. It is also that of a man who stands at the centre of an administrative machine the working of which is conditioned by the notion, or rather by the effects in practice, of Ministerial responsibility. The *préfet*, as the servant of all Ministers, the chief man of his *département*, but a subordinate point in a number of nation-wide administrations, is in a different and in some ways more complex position.[1]

The *préfet* has as immediate assistants, a sort of private office, with a *chef de cabinet* who is a junior member of the Prefectoral Corps, various *bureaux* which do the main routine work of the prefecture, and a *secrétaire général* who ranks as a *sous-préfet* and is, under the *préfet*, the chief administrative official of the prefecture and generally ensures its smooth internal working. By

[1] For a fuller account of the functions of the *préfet*, and a different assessment of his importance, see Brian Chapman, *The Prefects and Provincial France* (1955).

no means, however, are all the officials of importance in the *département* to be found in the prefecture or the *sous-préfectures*. The prefect lives surrounded by a variety of administrations. The British system is, by comparison, of a Napoleonic logic and simplicity. It is often said that in the eighteenth century France had become a confusion of authorities with overlapping areas of control. A hundred and fifty years after the Revolution she is certainly in that position. Every Frenchman is bound to tell you sooner or later that his country has *l'esprit cartésien*, one of the implications being that she has a passion for making a clean slate and designing a logical structure to replace what has been erased. Nothing could less accurately convey the spirit of French administrative reform. It is indeed impossible to achieve radical reform without more power and coherence than French governments have had for many years. If Napoleon approached the Cartesian ideal, there have been too many little Cartesians since for the result to show much of the logic on which the French pride themselves. The idea that the prefect could, by the exercise of mere authority, make good the deficiencies of the administrative system, is one not likely to appeal to the student of administration. Napoleon's more orthodox idea was to put the right men in place in a good system. A man of parts can get something out of a bad system, but a lack of simplicity and intelligibility is inadequately compensated by individual talent. The administrative systems which surround the prefect hardly enable him to exercise his abilities to the best advantage. They certainly do not enable him to live up to his theoretical rôle as the general representative of the government in his area.

It is not that the prefect has any competitor for this post. No one in the *département* has his finger in so many pies. The prefect's *chefs de division* appear between them to control everything. In fact, however, most of these divisions are concerned with legislation which is not only made in Paris but is designed to be administered on a national scale. As the representative in the department of all Ministers, the prefect is theoretically empowered to deal with it. It can even be argued that, in view of the excessive specialization which characterizes the central administration, a man of the prefect's general experience can

inject a little common sense into what is proposed or com-
manded from Paris. If that were true it would merely show the
prefect as an inadequate brake on a bad system, or as one of two
wrongs which still do not make an administrative right. In
practice the men at the centre are generally working on more
rational or, what passes for the same thing, more modern lines.
The prefect can, in many matters, do no more than meddle. He
may take things out of straightforward day-to-day administration for reasons irrelevant to the responsible Ministers, whose
real representatives are the senior local officials of their own
Ministries and the specialist staff responsible to those officials.
A prefect might well intervene to stop the prosecution for fraud
of a local notable whom the central administration and its
servants would certainly have pursued; he will hardly intervene
to ensure that the intention of certain legislation is being
properly carried out. He may, occasionally, by using his prestige,
that 'touch of authority' supposed to be dear, bring to a conclusion, in the right sense, a negotiation with which the
specialized services have struggled without final success. This
can happen in industrial conciliation, where the determining
factor, it can safely be said, is not a nostalgia for a vanished
authority but the well-known habit of hagglers not to give in
before the highest authority to which they have access has been
reached. If the prefect was not there, someone more expert
would be the highest authority.

The prefect may, of course, play a useful rôle in problems
which are of a local character but which involve various Ministries. For these matters he is the natural chairman. In this
country the chairman would be determined—and generally
quite without difficulty—by the subject matter of the problem.
The Ministry most concerned would take the chair. It may be
that such arrangements are facilitated, with us, by a somewhat
greater readiness to agree among ourselves than the French
can generally show, or a greater readiness to be bored by the
argument to which disagreement can give rise. The consultations in this country would, on any important question,
be regional rather than more narrowly local. This brings
us to one of the *cruces* of the prefectoral problem. It is evi-
dent that, for most of the major problems of government,

The Administrator as Governor

the department is an altogether inadequate unit. Most of the Ministries which need an organization in the provinces in fact work on a larger scale. Their regional territories do not have the same boundaries; the Ministries do not all have the same number of regions. A modest reform to be hoped for would be some alignment between them. That, however, would leave unsolved the problem of the relation between the Ministries and the prefect.[1] It was the reactionary government of Vichy which first tried to put the prefectoral system on a regional footing. Like other works of Vichy, it had to be undone. In 1948 posts of inspector-general of the administration were created with a competence extending over several departments. This reform, like that of Vichy, sprang from a concern for public order, and the regions of the inspectors-general are aligned with the military areas. The inspector-general could be and occasionally is of great utility. The inspector-general is, in the language of the people, a *super-préfet*, and the people is no doubt in the right of it as compared with the Ministry of the Interior's more discreet term. The *super-préfet* is better able to deal with the regional officers of the Ministries than is the prefect. He is more nearly the right size. But the same general objections hold good against him as against the prefect. There is no system or logic about the relationship between the frontiers of his territories and those of the Ministries; he cannot do anything that the representatives of the Ministries, agreeing among themselves could not do. He has not the advantage the prefect has of being *dans les moeurs*, with the force of tradition behind him, but there is no doubt that he is potentially the more useful official, an official more suited to the needs of the time. His very success, however, might lead to the continuance of a prefectoral system which can hardly be said to be an administrative necessity. It might prevent the decay of the prefect who, with a long period without the obsession of public order, might well attain the status and dignity of a Lord Lieutenant.

In a sense, the whole question turns on the preoccupation with public order which has, for reasons which the recent history of France make only too plain, been obsessive. The constitution

[1] No doubt things would be tidier if France had had to organize herself for total war.

89

of 1946 envisaged the department as run by an elected official, as it might be by the chairman of the county council. The laws applying this provision of the constitution have never been voted, and the reasons for this failure include a legitimate fear that, under a communist chairman, there might be danger even of a departmental separatism. There is a lack of confidence among the French in the possibility of a political solution of any such difficulty, and a preference for relying on an administrative solution. A long history of inadequate political direction, combined with a tradition inherited from an absolute monarchy, had led the French to look to the *fonctionnaire*, and above all to this strange half-political *fonctionnaire*, the prefect, to secure the coherence of the state. It is hardly for a foreigner to call in question the efficacy, in this matter, of the sober building in the *chef-lieu* of the department. There is no doubt that that building does represent, for the ordinary Frenchman, public order. And yet one cannot help wondering whether this conception of public order is not a trifle parochial, an affair of *gendarmes*, having little relation to economic forces that move the country.

The presence, in the Departments, of officials whose job is to carry out the will of the central government, is no more than is essential if there is to be any government at all. The prefect, however, like his opposite number in Spain and elsewhere, is something different in kind from the merely necessary official of a central administration. He is an official who, to use Gambetta's distinction, is *quelqu'un* as well as *quelque chose*, a politician as well as an administrator, and one may wonder whether an official of this type is altogether suited to the needs of a modern democracy. He is embedded in the administrative machine, and with the recruitment of a proportion of the prefectoral corps through the *Ecole Nationale d'Administration* he may well come to feel himself as more and more of it. But in reality he is a bit of the political mind of the country, a bit of political grit in the administrative machine. The mere fact that his appointment is revocable at any time and that his continuance in office is dependent on his political acceptability will separate him from the permanent officials. The fact that he is equipped, like a Minister, with a sort of private office which is apt to take a hand in matters as soon as they begin to smell slightly political, will ensure that the political aspect of the affairs dealt with by the administrative divisions is not lost sight of and may even cause it to be exaggerated. In this country the politics of any new legislation is generally lost sight of in the execution. This is probably largely true in France, where the social legislation, for example, is now *dans les moeurs* and accepted as much as the habit of political intervention is accepted. But the prefectoral system does in a measure keep the politics of things alive in the heart of the administration. Above all, it provides a ready opening for interventions based, as such things generally are, not on political principles but on political associations.[1] The French, particularly in the south, are passionately interventionist, and a great deal of time must be wasted in explaining the inevitability of administrative decisions, even when the intervention does not secure its object of effecting a deviation in the exercise of authority. This could of course be called educating public opinion.

It is unlikely that the cruder manifestations of the presence of a political official are much in evidence or extremely deleterious. The prefect has to please a lot of people, almost everyone except perhaps Poujadistes and Communists, and the more people he has to please the more nearly his circumspection will approach that of the ordinary administrator. Even so, the prefect will hardly be open to influences of the same generality as the pure administrator under the control of a central department would be. It is here that the local character of the prefect appears. The fact that he has so many masters—the fact that he is the representative of all the Ministers and not merely of the Minister of the Interior who no doubt has his first loyalty and to whom he sends a monthly report—must give him more independence than an official who has only one. His pressing concern is that all should go well, and above all that nothing should seem to go wrong, in his department. *Pas d'histoires!* His first impulse will be to strangle at birth any project likely

---

[1] It is amusing to recall, in this connection, Tocqueville's remarks about those who, under the *ancien régime*, demanded of the *intendant* 'that in their case the rules should be waived, and demand it just as imperiously as if they were asking that the rules should be followed.' Tocqueville (Paris, 1952), p. 135.

to give trouble to powerful local interests, and he will be tempted to abet the latter when they find themselves opposed to a national policy, a situation which puts a new gloss on the monarchic formula: '*Ordonne en outre Sa Majesté que toutes les contestations qui pourront survenir sur l'exécution du présent arrêt, circonstances et dépendances, seront portées devant l'intendant.*'[1] The instrument of Napoleonic centralization has become in a manner a focus for a kind of discreet decentralization, for a propping up of the departmental unit much as the individual citizen seeks to prop himself up against the ravages of the tax collector. Above all the prefect, while jealous of his rights as the first official of the department, does not want to do anything unpopular, or unpleasant to the influences that matter. If anything unpleasant has to be done he would rather some less public figure took the responsibility. '*C'est la politique du parapluie.*'

Viewed from the point of view of British *moeurs*, it is absurd to have an official in an admiral's uniform to get the work of the government done. Admittedly a prefect does not normally wear these garments when he is talking business, but in this country the mere knowledge that an official had such a get-up hidden away in his wardrobe would tell against him. The Lord Lieutenant is allowed to dress up because he has no authority to speak of. We have retained the splendour at the centre of loyalty but prefer not to be dazzled by those we are going to talk to. The French, having abolished the crown, are said by some Frenchmen to like a touch of authority. One may always suspect those who make assertions of this nature of liking themselves to exercise authority. There are however those who see in that exercise the most legitimate function of the prefect. It may be, in the vicissitudes France has known, that it has been; and it may be that some local stiffening of this sort is still required in a democracy so much less strongly led than ours, and with a general administration less integrated and more in love with its own academic and legal inventions. The hundred little men of authority in the *départements* may be thought of as battling against the fissiparity of the French party system and the subtilizings of the logicians at the Palais-Royal.

[1] Tocqueville, p. 123.

CHAPTER VIII

Centralization and Politics in Germany and Sweden

Without ever having had an administrative system, like the French, specifically designed to achieve centralization, England —one hardly dares, in this context, to say Britain—is, as a mere consequence of the political system, in fact highly centralized. Ministers have to answer in Parliament for their Departments; the Parliamentary Question and the Adjournment Debate are devices which ensure a remarkable degree of watchfulness over the doings of the administration. They influence far more than the matters to which they are at any one moment being applied. The administrator works in public in the sense that any of his actions, or the actions of any other official with whom he is connected, may at any time have to be explained in Parliament in terms that will satisfy members. This sense of the publicity of his actions is genuine and lively; it is sometimes underrated by people whose inside knowledge of the Civil Service is limited to the years of war, a time of unusual individual initiatives and of muted public criticism. The mode of political control determines the extent and nature of the centralization which is characteristic of the service. That centralization is a direct consequence of Ministerial responsibility. Various devices may be adopted to establish in outstations uniform routines which will ensure that what goes on is on lines which the Minister is seized of and can depend on, but any decentralization of policy is impossible without derogating from Ministerial responsibility and taking the business out of the field of Parliamentary supervision. Centralization is in the logic of any administrative system as such; it is also, and forcibly, in the logic of parliamentary democracy.

There is a sense in which it may be said that in all countries day-to-day administration escapes the eye of the politician, and in which this is a good and healthy thing. But to cut such administration off from political influences is desirable only in the measure that the political system is a bad one. A bureaucracy not responsive to the political pressures and tendencies of the age soon dies. What is needed to keep it healthy is a regular and general pressure from public opinion, for which the political power should act as a focus. When people congratulate themselves on the relative independence of the administrative organization from political control it is either because of a feeling that the political intervention they would be likely to get would be irregular and representative of particular rather than of general influences, or because, as officials themselves, they like to see the growth of their own *imperium in imperio*.

In Spain it is frankly admitted that this quasi-independence of the administration is conditional on its not impinging on political matters. This is a large qualification. It means that if administrator and *administré* think the right thoughts no harm will come to them. On that understanding of the matter, the Spanish 'independence' looks rather like what in England we should call servility. In France a thing is taken out of the normal run of the administration's cares (perhaps at this point being transferred from the specialized service to the prefect's own *cabinet*) on the factual ground that a deputy or other politician is interested in it and is working all the magic he knows to get it settled as he wants. Spain no doubt enjoys all the pleasures and inconveniences of that kind of interventionism, and the fifty provincial governors are there to do all the prefect does (and perhaps more): in addition, there is the watch for heresy, in this country of the Inquisition, which gives all politically-minded persons a chance for intervention which would not exist in France. For, in Spain, 'to be liberal, that is to say heretical, is worse than to be an assassin, a thief or an adulterer. The worst sin is not to obey the Church [or indeed the state], whose infallibility [the state's also] forbids us the use of reason.' So Miguel de Unamuno,[1] in 1912—a statement true after as well as long before that date.

[1] Miguel de Unamuno, *Del Sentimiento Trágico de la Vida*, fourth edition (1941), p. 64.

The Spanish official's suggestion that the British administration is characteristically that of a country in which the executive has been defeated by the legislature, is based on a false distinction between the political and the official executive, which are not two powers but one, even though certain defects in their nervous systems may lead, on occasions, to a certain dichotomy of outlook and action. Some of these defects in the nervous system are to be seen in our set-up, but they are under permanent treatment because any Minister can, at any moment, be called upon to defend publicly any action of his officials. This is an obligation which can hardly be said to rest on Ministers in Spain, and even in France a Minister may, if only to a very limited extent, perhaps reluctantly unload his responsibility on to the *Conseil d'Etat*.

A discontinuity between the political and official executives, and a discontinuity between central government and out-stationed administrations, are equally incompatible with the British doctrine of Ministerial responsibility. Some of the consequences of such discontinuities can be seen in the German and Swedish systems of administration which, in quite different ways, rest constitutionally on there being clean breaks in the chain which extends from Ministers to the *administré*. In the Swedish system, most of the routine administration is entrusted to agencies, as if a clear line could be drawn showing the point at which the Ministers' responsibilities end. The German system is, of course, federal, and the political background of it is not a little complicated.

The justifications for the establishment of the post-war German Federation were at least as good as such things usually are. The dismemberment of Germany was, for understandable reasons, viewed with favour by many Frenchmen. For the British the question must be considered to have been too high-brow, but one can imagine that to Americans, even those without any brows at all, a federal system might easily seem to be a thing enshrined in natural law. The views of the occupying powers, however, made an infinitesimal contribution to this matter as compared with contribution made by German history and tradition. The second Roman empire was more notable for its particularism than for its holiness; the world of Goethe was

Centralization and Politics

a world of, so to speak, village notables. From 1871 to 1934 Germany was in law a federal state, and until 1918 there was only one Reichsminister—the Chancellor. With few exceptions such as foreign affairs and the post office, the whole administration was carried out by the member states of the federation, the *Länder*, even though the laws might often be *Reich* laws. When *Reich* authorities began to be built up, they were at first specialized authorities only, for such matters as the post and unemployment insurance. Hans Peters draws attention to the significance of the establishment, in 1919, of the central tax administration. 'With that,' he says, 'the Reich for the first time set up, outside the general administrative field of the *Länder*, an organization of its own divided up into central, intermediate and local authorities.'[1] The rule of the Nazis brought the independence of the *Länder* to an end, and the anti-Nazi enthusiasm of the postwar years, less ferocious but not always less blind than the fury it replaced, would no doubt have ensured, if nothing else had done, that even what might otherwise have been regarded as a harmless bit of administrative tidying up should, since it was the work of the Nazis, be revised. The tidying up had not been undertaken in accordance with the best administrative manners. On 7 April 1933 special commissioners[2] were put in by the Führer to keep an eye on the *Länder* governments, and although a few months afterwards the Land parliaments were magicked away the commissioners remained and became established as regular regional authorities. If a Land was not important enough to deserve the whole attention of one of these eminent officials it was grouped with one or two others to make a convenient region. Hitler's empire, unlike Napoleon's, did not need a system of prefects each ruling over a little territory to the frontiers of which they could ride on a horse in a day. There were no general Reich authorities below the level of the commissioners. The police and what was called justice had been taken over by the Reich and these authorities of course pursued their specialities everywhere.

The feeling that Germany has not been at her best when she has, as during the Third Reich, abandoned the federal system

[1] Hans Peters, *Lehrbuch der Verwaltung*, p. 42.
[2] *Reichsstatthalter.*

or when, as during Bismarck's ascendancy, she was moving towards unification, has naturally given many Germans tender sentiments towards the federal system, and one could, certainly, sooner become tender towards Bavaria or even Rheinland-Pfalz than towards a greater Germany of whatever degree of completeness. The political aruguments for a federal Germany remain, though no doubt they do not seem as strong to a Social Democrat in the Bonn Parliament (*Bundestag*) as to Right-wing Roman Catholics in Bavaria. The country is anyhow bound by the constitution to the federal principle, and any administrative inconveniences of the system must be tolerated in the interest of more fundamental considerations. And quite a lot of administrative reorganization would be possible without the basic law being set aside. It would, for example, be possible to change the frontiers of the *Länder*. Those who believe in federation speak of it as a dynamic principle, which may be taken to be German for something which is not quite comfortable and will certainly change itself in time. Meanwhile, or perhaps for as long as any federal system may last, there is a Ministry for Federal Affairs (or rather for the Affairs of the Bundesrat), which is the seat of an internal diplomacy beside which that of the German Foreign Office must be child's play.

The *Bundesrat* itself is a senate the peculiar rules of whose operation reflect, no doubt, the controversies surrounding its creation. It is made up of members of the *Länder* governments, and in general the members have to take instructions from their governments, so that the *Länder* take a direct part in federal legislation. When the government introduces a draft law it sends it first of all to the *Bundesrat*, so that the reactions of the *Länder* governments are so far as possible known at this stage. No doubt they are in general known before this stage, for such a political consultation casts its shadow before in the form of administrative consultations between Federal and *Land* officials before the draft has seen the light of day. When the draft law first goes to the nationally elected *Bundestag* it goes accompanied by any amendments proposed by the *Bundesrat* and any counter-proposals the government may wish to put forward. If it survives the three readings in the *Bundestag* the bill goes back to the *Bundesrat*. At this point a remarkable change comes over the members of this august body. If they do not approve the law in the form in which the *Bundestag* likes it, they may, as members of a joint committee of *Bundestag* and *Bundesrat*, cease to be obstreperous devils representing the *Länder* governments they belong to and, as gentle poodles, give their own personal opinion, which has, of course, long been known to the Minister for Federal Affairs and his officials. It is in fact generally possible for the joint committees to agree. There is a further legislative complication between *Land* and Federation, for the latter authority, sometimes referred to as the 'woman who is only a top part',[1] has a brain of the greatest complexity. The basic law distinguishes between ordinary laws and those which need the agreement of the *Bundesrat*. For the latter, the *Bundesrat* acts as a genuine second chamber, and if it does not agree the *Bundestag's* determination is null and void. But for the ordinary laws, if there is no agreement after the whole of the procedure outlined has been completed, the *Bundesrat* is simply overruled by the *Bundestag*, that is to say that the *Länder* disappear before the superior power of the Federation.

The strains and stresses between Federation and *Länder* already provide a difficult legislative context for the administration. The consultations between Federation and *Länder* officials which take place when a draft federal law is being prepared no doubt serve to bring the experience of the *Länder* into the making of the law; still more, no doubt, they bring their particularist demands. The situation is not necessarily any funnier than that which exists between certain Departments in Britain and the local authorities, but it certainly looks as if it would give rise to greater difficulties. The status of our central government is unquestioned; that of the Federation is much more doubtful. While the most important legislation is, with the qualifications which have been explained, federal legislation, the general receptacle of power, so to speak, is the *Länder*, which have under the basic law the reversion of any powers not specifically given to the Federation. Their status, both by the constitution and by tradition, is thus something quite unknown in this country. Moreover, while the field of operation of our local authorities is restricted, and many Departments have a

---

[1] 'die Frau ohne Unterleib'—a phrase which has had some currency in Bonn.

strong regional organization of their own, the Federation is in its regional and local organization remarkably restricted. There is a whole range of administrative Departments[1] in Bonn without dependencies in the provinces. Indeed, the regional organization is practically confined to certain almost extra-governmental activities such as the running of the post and railways and the customs. The only system of regional organization which exists in the general administration is in the field of finance, and in this matter the connection between *Bund* and *Land* looks somewhat tenuous and it is generally held, in Bonn, that the control is inadequate. The Finance Ministry has a number of Finance Directorates which are made up in the main of *Länder* officials but include two small sections staffed by federal officials which deal with customs, turnover tax and certain other federal matters. The real link is provided by the official who rules this agglomeration.[2] He is a juridically curious animal, half federal official and half *Land* official, and he risks enjoying the complete confidence of neither master. Certainly he is too thin a bridge to carry all that should flow between the outer and the inner ring of the administration. There is impotence in Bonn, because the laws are made there but the *Länder* governments carry them out, and because the Federation has to find the money and the *Länder* spend it. This distrust between the parts of what, despite all constitutional appearances and complications, is after all a national administration, not only itself hinders free communication but creates conditions in which the confidence may grow even less. Something more than a mere passion for the law incites the Federal Finance Ministry to put in the most detailed legal form everything related to the expenditure of money by the *Länder* which can be so put. 'What is not put down in black and white, in a law, does not exist.' It is a symptom of distrust. The Federation pursues an agonized legal perfectionism, with one eye on the taxi-meter; the *Länder* lay claim to more enlightened views in the hope that the vagueness of enlightenment will enable them to spend more.

[1] The whole structure of the administration in Federation and *Länder* is comprehensively set out in Harry von Rosen-von Hoewel, *Allgemeines Verwaltungsrecht* (1957, Schaeffers Grundriss des Rechts und der Wirtschaft, 29 Band, I Teil) pp. 44–65.
[2] The *Oberfinanzpräsident*.

Centralization and Politics

There are those who favour any interference with the power of a central authority, as part of the Manichaean battle between the light of the individual and the darkness of the state. In the case of Germany, there are still a few who favour the federal system because they think it will keep her weak. Both this theology and this politics are equally irrelevant to the administrative problem raised by this particular federal system. The administrative problem is to ensure that enough administrative experience gets into the legislation to make it workable, and that, once made, the legislation should be carried out in the spirit in which it was conceived by the central authority which passed it. To an outsider there would seem, in the present German system, to be difficulties on both these scores. It is true that the *Bundesrat*, and the Ministry for Federal Affairs, are so constituted and operated as to ensure that the point of view of the *Länder* is not overlooked when legislation is being drafted. Almost any legislation, in any country, comes out of the pushing and thrusting of many pressures. But there should be a sizeable administrative forum, within a Ministry, at the stage when a draft project is submitted to Ministers for their sanction or disapproval, where the various pressures can be weighed and measured and a reasonably objective *compte rendu* prepared. One may be left with the suspicion that, in Germany, the pressures press a little too closely in on the final stages of preparing a draft law, and the room for dispassionate consideration is a little too small. Whether or not this is so—and the amount of play for dispassionate consideration will vary, in the best-administered countries, with the politics of the enactment and of the moment—there seems to be little doubt that the provisions for ensuring that legislation, once passed, is carried out in the spirit in which it was devised, are quite inadequate. There is virtually no administrative control of what the *Länder* are doing. Everything turns on their taste for loyalty to the Federation, or, shall we say, for subordination to Bonn. Towards Bonn they are, however, in the classic position of Lyautey longing for '*le grand coup de hache décentralisateur*',[1] and the hatchet they have is, from Bonn's point of view, an uncomfortably sharp one. They are certainly in a position to resume, so far as the text of a

[1] Lyautey, *Choix de Lettres, 1882–1919* (1947), p. 68.

law allows, any struggles they lost when the law was being drafted. They are in effect provincial administrations headed by politicians, and there must inevitably be some uncertainty as to whether they are political or, in the narrower sense, administrative bodies. It is a significant fact that that co-ordination which in a centralized system would be sought by regular meetings of the controlling regional officers concerned at the headquarters of the Ministry is replaced, in the case of Ministry of Labour, by three-monthly meetings of *Länder* Ministers of Labour, convened in turn by one of the *Land* Ministers and with the convening Minister in the chair. The Federal Minister of Labour may attend as a guest, and although the *Länder* Ministers bring one or more officials with them the Federal Minister chooses not to do so.

It is generally supposed that the very efficiency and obedience of the German official have been excessive in the past and that a little disorder would improve the system.

> *Durch wenig Interpunktion,*
> *Durch plötzliches Etcetera*
> *Und grosse Subordination*
> *Kam seinem Heer die Flucht zu nah.*[1]

An administration is, however, an instrument with which one can do all kinds of things, good or bad, and it is not certain that any good cause will be furthered by impediments in the admini-stration. Some further centralization—probably first of all in the field of financial administration—there will certainly have to be. A centralized and relatively impersonal administration is so far from being undemocratic that it is, indeed, one of the marks of modern social democracy, while the administration of the Reich and of Prussia entrusted many tasks to subordinate authorities.

This generalization about the administrative requirements of social democracy might seem to be belied by the case of Sweden. Sweden is, indeed, a country of which the student of administration may tell strange tales. The Ministries are tiny, and the Civil Servants, unlike their secretive brothers else-where, lay their papers guilelessly before a critical and enlight-ened populace. It is an idyllic picture.

[1] Clemens Brentano, *Die Rheinmärchen.*

Centralization and Politics

A Swedish Ministry may have a staff of, say, forty or fifty people including everyone from the equivalent of the Permanent Secretary to the typists, and the total staff of the ten[1] Ministries is only about six hundred. The whole lot lumped together would not make up the numbers of a small British Ministry. The population of Great Britain is something like six times that of Sweden, but even if one multiplies the six hundred by six one still barely reaches the total of a middle-sized British Ministry. The most immoderate critic of the British service would hesitate to ascribe these differences to the length of tea-breaks in Whitehall. The differences are, in fact, due to differences of function as between the Swedish Ministries and our own. While our Ministries characteristically attend to everything, from the widest issues of policy to the most out-of-the-way individual case, for which, under the British political system, Ministers may be held responsible in Parliament, and some of the biggest include very large regional and local staffs, the Swedish Ministries are in effect merely secretariats gathered around their Ministers. It looks as if the Swedes had succeeded in isolating the essential Ministerial functions so that Ministers and senior officials could move in a luminous atmosphere in which issues of policy are uncomplicated by administrative details. Ministers and senior officials in this country might well sigh for such an immunity from petty care.

If the language of purpose could be used in this connection, one might indeed say that the object of the Swedish system was to remove from the centre of government most of the details that ordinarily encumber such centres. In Sweden, most of the day-to-day administration which in our system is the pre-occupation of Ministries is not carried out by Ministries at all but by separate administrative agencies. This it is, of course, which accounts for the small size of the staffs of the Ministries; the administrative agencies, of which .there are a considerable number, employ between them some thousands of people.[2] This decentralization of administration into the hands of agencies

---

[1] This excludes the Ministry of Foreign Affairs, the staff of which is greater than that of all the others put together—just over 1,000.

[2] According to official statistics the total number of agencies is over 250 and they employ between them about 220,000 people. These figures, however, include

is not, however, the result of a reform designed as a solution of the difficulties known to attend on central control in a modern socialized state. It is of much older growth and, if it could be said to solve those problems, that would be a happy accident. The agencies are the direct descendants of boards provided for in the Instrument of Government of 1634. These boards were intended as departments of government in much the sense in which we should use that term. There were five of them, each under one of the great officers of state, and they were originally supposed to be equal in status. In time, however, the board headed by the Chancellor 'developed into a number of different Ministries, working directly with the King, whereas the other four boards . . . branched off into a great number of new agencies. But the Chancery, which remained the common name for all Ministries taken together, did on the other hand not acquire any definite ascendancy over the other boards . . . the original boards and the agencies which had branched off from them retained their independence of the Ministries. . . . The King alone maintained the right to give orders to these authorities; the Minister could speak only through the King and in so far as the King—or, later, the government as a whole—was willing to support him.'[1] This, then, is the general shape of the Swedish administration; the day-to-day work done by a large number of administrative agencies, central and local, which constitutionally are not the mere subordinates of Ministries or even responsible to a Minister, but are responsible to the government as a whole, the Ministries 'as a rule . . . not (being) authorized to take individual administrative decisions'.[2] It is a picture to delight anyone fond enough to imagine that all the evils of the modern state somehow stem from Ministries. To the student of administration it looks like confusion, and, it may be added, the system does not appear to offer any great hope of effective public control, though, to be sure, the supposed guilelessness of Swedish officials in laying their papers before the public might be expected to look after that.

military and local administration, government enterprises, academies and museums. The number of central agencies proper can be put at around 50 and the number of staff at 7,000.

[1] Gunnar Heckscher, *Swedish Public Administration at Work* (1955) (issued by Studieförbundet Näringsliv och Samhälle) p. 6.   [2] Heckscher, p. 6.

Centralization and Politics

The relationships between the executive and the legislature, in this famous social democracy of the north, are, oddly enough, in essentials fixed by a hundred-and-fifty-year-old document which was, in Professor Heckscher's words, partly designed to safeguard 'the independence of the executive branch of government from encroachment by parliament'.[1] This is the Instrument of Government of 1809.[2] Sweden had experienced, from 1720 to 1772, an 'Era of Liberty' which had been followed by a period of absolutism, and the Instrument of Government, which came into being after the deposition of Gustaf IV Adolf following his defeat by the Russians, was an attempt at a compromise between the two systems. The document provides that 'The King alone shall govern the realm', but that he shall, in certain specified instances, 'seek the information and advice of a Council of State' (Article 4). The limitations imposed on the activity of parliament are striking:

'Matters relating to the appointment and removal of officials, the decisions, resolutions and judgments of the executive or judicial authorities, the affairs of private citizens and corporations, or the execution of any law, statute, or regulations,shall in no case or manner be subject to consideration by the Riksdag, its houses, or committees, except as literally prescribed in the fundamental laws'—(Article 90).

The principle embodied in this article is, says Heckscher, 'on the whole maintained in practice, and even questions in parliament never have the same bearing upon administrative work as they do in Great Britain'.[3] This is, certainly, parliamentary government with limitations which would not for a moment be tolerated in Westminster.

The British Civil Servant is, historically and constitutionally, a nonentity, strictly the servant of a Minister, and a man whose every action is liable to question at any moment in Parliament. The heads of the Swedish administrative system are the heirs of a largely autocratic system and as such enjoy still a measure

[1] Heckscher, p. 8.
[2] The text of the Instrument of Government, as amended up to and including the year 1953, is given in an English translation, in *The Constitution of Sweden* (Documents published by the Royal Ministry for Foreign Affairs), Stockholm, (1953), p. 11 ff.
[3] Heckscher, p. 8.

of freedom from democratic control. It is against this background that the principle of the publicity of official documents is to be understood. The basic law on this subject, is to be found in Chapter 2 of the Freedom of the Press Act,[1] the object of which is said to be 'to further free interchange of opinion and general enlightenment' (Article 1.). The law covers 'all documents kept by a State or local government authority, whether received or prepared by such an authority' (Article 2). All such documents have to be made available to any Swedish subject who asks to see them, unless they are of a class specifically excepted by law. There are some important exceptions to the general rule, not only in the field of defence and foreign affairs, certain police matters and certain social and tax matters involving information of a personal character, but in all fields whatever so far as working papers are concerned. While a matter is still under consideration an official can, in general, plead that he needs the document, though he may undoubtedly, in certain cases, be put by journalists under serious pressure to release it. There is a certain understandable vagueness among officials as to what they in fact regard as working papers. Personal letters passing between officials have been authoritatively held to be official documents, but there is no doubt that such letters continue to pass not infrequently as if they were not. Even notes of telephone conversations may be regarded as within the scope of the law, but unrecorded telephone conversations play an important part in the technique of living with this law as an administrator. The law contains one provision which the hard-pressed administrator must certainly regard as beneficent:

'A memorandum or other note' (so runs Article 4), 'drawn by an authority solely to present or prepare a case or matter for decision shall not be deemed to be an official document in the hands of such authority unless, after the case or matter has been settled by the authority, the note is placed on permanent record.'

This is an open invitation to edit papers before they become liable to be made public, and is presumably used where necessary to keep from the public eye the pros and cons of the argument

[1] *The Constitution of Sweden*, p. 82 ff.

that went on within an office before a decision was reached. Moreover, since with a matter of policy it is often difficult to determine when the end is reached, there may be supposed to be here some room for manoeuvre. The law on the public character of official documents is most effectively operated away from the centres of political power. It may be invoked, certainly, by a journalist wanting to get hold of a report which he knows has been presented to a Ministry by some outside agency. Within the Ministries themselves it may be regarded as a dead letter—or as something that has just as much life as the authorities concerned want it to have. On the work of the agencies it probably exercises a genuine and in general probably not unwholesome influence, though it may sometimes desensitize the channels of communication between one administrative unit and another in a manner which must be suspected of producing a measure of insubordination, inefficiency and waste. It may, in any case, be regarded as a valuable additional check in a system in which parliamentary control is, by our standards, deficient.

A further check on the working of the administration is to be found in the persons of the two Procurators (one for Civil and one for Military Affairs) appointed by the Riksdag under Article 96 of the Instrument of Government. These procurators, acting 'in the capacity of representatives of the Riksdag . . . supervise the observance of laws and statutes as applied . . . by the courts and by public officials and employees' (Article 96). A private citizen cannot take an official into court, but he can complain to the Procurator who may do so if he thinks the complaint justified such action. In practice the Procurator, on receiving a complaint, will make informal enquiries which do not necessarily go on the record, rather as the Comptroller and Auditor-General may do with us, and proceed to more formal action only if he is sure of his ground. The existence of the Procurator is felt as a genuine and lively check far exceeding in importance that of the cases he actually takes to court; and the Procurator's influence is, of course, apt to be used on the side of those wishing to obtain the publication of documents.

While the aristocratic traditions of Swedish administration have to some extent been tempered by the publicity given to documents and by the activities of the Procurator for Civil Affairs, public control also makes itself felt by political means. The existence of a parliament, whatever its constitutional limitations, will inevitably tend to produce a demand for such control. The theory of Swedish administration, as we have seen, is that the heads of agencies are independent of Ministers and answerable only to the government as a whole. In a complex administration this would be an unwieldy arrangement, and it would seem that mere pressure of business at the centre would result in the agencies being left free to go their own way within, of course, the limits imposed by the law. If a Minister could not decide even an individual case without taking the matter to the cabinet, would he not often be prevented from making his views felt? In fact, if someone appeals[1] to the government against the decision of an agency—which is possible in a number of cases, although not in all—the matter is effectively settled by the Ministry concerned. It is true that the question has formally to be put to the government, but this is done at the Friday meetings of the King in Council at which some hundreds of cases may be disposed of in half an hour, so that the government assumes responsibility without anyone outside the Ministry concerned knowing what is involved. In a more general way, it may be said that Ministers effectively exercise over the agencies with which they are concerned the control formally vested in the government as a whole by virtue of the fact that they enjoy the confidence of their colleagues, or more simply, on the good cabinet principle that Ministers sink or swim together. Heckscher uses what seems to the outside observer excessively cautious language on this matter of the relationships between Ministries and agencies. 'Ministers themselves might'. he says, 'occasionally find it useful to attempt to put a little judicious pressure on an agency which is in danger of becoming too independent. This is one of the points,' he adds fairly enough, 'where the actual facts of the situation are not very easy to establish.'[2] There is no doubt, however, that the Ministries do not wait for the formalities of a government decision where the case is urgent and they feel sure of their ground. Moreover,

[1] Appeals are possible only when the appellant has a formal *locus standi.*
[2] Heckscher, p. 17.

they have meetings with agencies at which it is made clear to the latter what the course of government policy will be and it is not unknown for a Ministry to ask an agency to see the draft of a memorandum which is later to be submitted to it formally and steps might be taken to ensure that such a document is not treated as public, though this would no doubt depend on the goodwill of the head of the agency which, in a country where officials have full freedom of political acitvity, could not always be counted on.

The Swedish system is at many important points so different from our own that the British administrator is surprised to find himself so much at home in it. The fact that he does perhaps points to the basic unimportance of administrative devices as compared with what one might call the temper of the administration. Sweden is ethnographically and culturally a simpler land than ours, but one cannot fail to recognize a certain kinship in the sober and practical turn of mind in which the Swedes approach their affairs. There is something in it of our own disregard of theory and of our slowness to change, in what is called a logical fashion, old things that can perfectly well be adapted to new needs. The Kingdom of Sweden, the Goths and the Wends has been turned into a modern social democracy in spite of the stiff joints of its constitutional administration. The peculiarities of the Swedish system are rather disadvantages which have been overcome than pointers for the organization of a modern administration. And no one, one imagines, would wish to impose on a country with a more fortunate political history the complexities of the German system. Neither system can be said to show up to disadvantage our narrow union of political and administrative power.

CHAPTER IX

The Politician as Intruder

It is possible for the political and administrative authorities in this country to act as effectively as a single power for the very reason that there is so sharp a differentiation of function between them, because, in short, there are no administrative *authorities* but only administrative instruments used by the political power. This differentiation is by no means to be taken for granted. It is least marked in those régimes which have a tradition of the Civil Servant as governor, and it is precisely in the case of such officials as the *préfet* that the danger of their being at cross-purposes with the political power is most feared. An English authority on the prefectoral system, speaking of 'the events of 1940 and 1944', says that they 'confirm, if that was necessary, that the Prefect's place in the administration of the country is of such importance that a real change in political direction must be accompanied by a profound modification in the composition of the corps. This, to the French, appears reasonable.'[1] Both 1940 and 1944 were years of revolution and it is natural that, at such times, the governing politician should be alarmed about what the governing official might get up to. Although the possible dichotomy of the political and administrative powers, resulting from the imperfect differentiation of their functions, gives most cause for anxiety in times of violent change, the anxiety is not confined to such times and is indeed endemic in the system. Hence, of course, the special insecurity of tenure of such officials as the *préfet*. Chapman's comment, which is illuminating, is no doubt intended to have a wide application:

'The selfless administrator', he goes on, 'without clear or

[1] Chapman, p. 157.

109

profound convictions is of little use either to a Government or to a society when called upon to deal with matters so fundamental as the control of education, police and industrial conflict.'[1]

This comes very near to equating 'clear and profound convictions' with the specific differences of opinion which are the stock-in-trade of politicians; an administrator might reply that there are national terms of reference, the common ground of parties, which may be held to not less firmly than the items of a party programme, though admittedly they are less clearly seen in a country which has undergone frequent changes of régime than in one which has been more fortunate. The British, anyhow, do not pay their officials to 'control education' nor to exercise their own opinions in the conflicts, industrial or other, that are played out upon the national stage. And it may be added that, in these matters, it is far from certain that the play of opinion is more effective than a long patience.

The British system rests on the obedience of the official or, if all systems may be said to do the same, one may fairly characterize our own as exhibiting a remarkable degree of mutual confidence as between politicians and officials. It is not suggested that French Ministers do not, in general, trust the officials in their Ministries to carry out the policies imposed on them from on high, but it is probably true that the relative instability of French governments gives high officials in that country a somewhat strong sense that the government rests on them and a consequent predisposition to nurse their private policies. It is hard for an outsider to judge such matters. A certain distrust of 'the selfless administrator' is, however, openly written into the administrative system of France, as into that of a number of other countries. The French Ministry is, in effect, divided into two interacting parts, a large neutral part and a small part of high political voltage. The neutral, stable element is made up of the *bureaux*, divided up, much like a British Ministry, into what in France are called *directions* and *sous-directions*. The political part is made up of the Minister's *cabinet*, and one might say that that institution is there to ensure that the permanent structure of the Ministry is sufficiently responsive to his direction. Up to 1940, there were really several *cabinets*: an office

1 Chapman, p. 157.

which received and registered correspondence and shared it out among the *bureaux*; sometimes a technical office made up of specialists; and finally the private secretaries doing a mixture of political work and routine office work.[1] The *cabinet* consists of people of the Minister's own choosing. Their number is fixed by law,[2] and, if the law does not prescribe their functions it is at least at pains to give each of them a general description. There is a *directeur* and a *chef du cabinet*; there are assistant *chefs*, a chief private secretary, and two people who in some sort act as specialist advisers—normally nine people in all. The appointment is a formal one, announced in the *Journal Officiel*. The members of the *cabinet* may be ordinary officials, but the law lays down only the minima of qualifications, or rather of disqualifications, namely that they must be people who have not been deprived of their civil rights and that their military service papers must be in order, and anyone may be chosen. They are, collectively, the dynamite with which the Minister, in the course of his peregrinations, enters a new establishment. But more gently, one might say that they are supposed to form a link between the Minister and the permanent administration. The scheme must be supposed to have some advantages in the contexts in which it is used, but it is probably better administratively not to interpose a body of trusties between the Minister and his Ministry. A Minister commands loyalty by virtue of his office, but it is difficult to believe that a band of wandering hangers-on does not arouse something more like suspicion and jealousy, and make the ground more fertile for intrigue. However that may be, the system inevitably creates a class of officials who follow the personal fortunes of Ministers in a way which is unknown in this country and which can hardly contribute to the smooth working of the administration. There are certain safeguards in the law.[3] Public officials called upon to serve in a Minister's *cabinet* may be promoted only in accordance with the rules governing promotion in the class to which they belong, but the situation is not without possibilities and the placing of ex-members of Ministers' *cabinets* in the prefectoral corps does not pass without jealous notice from their colleagues.

[1] Rolland, p. 163.   [2] Décret du 28 juillet 1948 (Code administratif).
[3] Décret du 13 juillet, 1911 (Code administratif).

111

The Politician as Intruder

The British administration enjoys an extraordinary degree of freedom from political intrusion, and there is no doubt that this freedom greatly facilitates the responsiveness of the administration to the purposes of cabinet government. The British administrator is able to be genuinely indifferent to the political colour of the government he serves because politicians accept constitutional limitation of their field of influence in a manner which is by no means to be taken for granted in countries outside Britain. The forbearance of British politicians is systematic, resting on the critical force of the opposition and on public opinion. It gives us, in contrast with what might fairly be described as the general system in Europe—or indeed in the world at large—permanent heads of Ministries who owe nothing to political connections and whose status is such that they can as a matter of course, without reference to political connections and subject only to Treasury concurrence which prevents more than a limited amount of departmental idosyncrasy, determine the *personnel*, or as the scarcely less inelegant usage of Whitehall has it, the establishments policies of their Ministries.

The German Civil Service of the Bismarckian Empire, which in some respects must have been exceedingly unlike the present Service in Whitehall, is said to have enjoyed an independence of political influence in its internal workings somewhat similar to that we still enjoy. Such independence is possible only under the shadow of a strong political *régime*. Theodor Eschenburg says of the old German service that it was 'socially one-sided, but it operated as a unity and in accordance with firm standards of quality. The much exaggerated class consciousness of this service corresponded to a high professional ethos and standard of performance. Neither political nor economic groups had influence on its establishments, not even the agrarian organizations.'[1] One has not to wander long in the corridors of Bonn to discover that things are not like that now. It is a long time since they have been exactly like that. Eschenburg puts the beginning of the modern patronage of office in 1921, when the political parties began to press for a quota of posts as a means, though it would seem an inadequate one, of securing a bureaucracy sensible of the needs of the new times. Hitler

[1] Theodor Eschenburg, *Herrschaft der Verbände?* (1955), p. 12.

hated the bureaucracy and tried to secure its dominance by *one* party, partly by planting or promoting sympathizers, partly by employing agents, sometimes among the messengers and drivers, who could keep an eye on their nominal masters. If the new politicians suspect the Civil Service, they are not in a particularly good tradition in doing so, nor in a particularly democratic one. And if the personnel has changed, so that one could say that something a little different was being suspected by each of the three régimes, the changes as between consecutive régimes have affected only a small, though admittedly important, proportion of officials. A modern state has need of its bureaucracy and is hardly more likely to lose the lot in a revulsion of public feeling than it is to lose the whole of its hospital or newspaper staffs.

The German official[1] is still, in his way, a proud creature. His preserve (as distinct from that of other employees or workers in the state service) in general includes all those administrative and executive posts which carry with them a bit of the authority of the state or of a public corporation, as well as all those more modest positions of trust, such as those of the postman, the railway-driver and the signalman, in which public safety is involved. The generic name for the tasks carrying with them a morsel of public authority is '*hoheitsrechtliche*'[2] activities. The etymology of the word '*hoheitsrechtliche*' is no doubt significant: '*Hoheit*', 'Highness', '*Hoheitsrecht*' 'royal prerogative'. The official is the successor of all those advisers and executants who flourished around the German courts of former times. This touch of what was once magic is probably, in these times, more damaging than helpful to the official's reputation with politicians and public. And yet if in one sense the politician may be said to distrust the officials and perhaps tends to be a

[1] There are three categories of state servant in Germany; the *Beamte*, or official proper, with whom we are here concerned; the *Arbeiter*, or worker, who corresponds, though not exactly, with the 'industrial' Civil Servant in Britain; and the intermediate class of *Angestellte* or employee. There is some overlapping of function as between *Beamte* and *Angestellte*; see von Rosen-von Hoewel, p. 37.

[2] According to the definition given by the German High Court, a *hoheitsrechtlich* activity is one involving the issue, by or on behalf of the state or a public corporation, of a duly authorized order or prohibition. *See* the official collection of decisions of the High Court (*Reichsgericht*), Vol. 93, p. 258. I am indebted to Professor Menger, of the Hochschule für Verwaltungswissenschaften Speyer, for this note.

113

little too desperately anxious to prove that he is commanding
and not taking advice, in another sense there tends to be, from
our point of view and indeed from that of some German critics,
an insufficient gap between officials and politicians. No single
feature of the arrangement is, to an Englishman, more striking
than the fact that the *Staatssekretär* (the equivalent of the Permanent Secretary) can and does deputise for his Minister in the
House. When he does so he may get into trouble either for not
putting forcefully enough all his Minister might have said or
for taking upon himself more than becomes a mere official, or
both.

The *Staatssekratär* is of course a political official, nominated
by or at any rate pleasing to his Minister. So are the *Mini-
sterialdirektors*, his lieutenants, who may be regarded as the
equivalent of our Under Secretaries. It is not to be supposed,
however, that political influence on establishments policy ends
there. It is of course impossible for an outsider, and perhaps not
always easy for an insider, to say exactly how far it does go and
what is involved in it. One cannot fail, however, to notice a
certain uneasiness in German officials on this point; either
urging that the extent of political influence has been much
exaggerated or openly regretting that it is there. The influence
is not only that of the parties directly but of other outside bodies
which, generally, make their influence felt through the politicians. One instance, taken from Eschenburg who offers a varied
selection, will show not merely outside influences at work considerably below the level of those appointments admitted to be
political but working in a manner which we should regard as the
grossest interference with a question of conscience. The case is
one of a candidate for promotion to a rank below the rank of
our 'principal'. He was a Roman Catholic, married to a Protestant, and he had allowed his children Protestant baptism, in
defiance, of course, of the Roman rule for mixed marriages.
The Minister was also a Roman Catholic and, it was expressly
said, could not answer for such a promotion. It is as if, in
England, an Anglican Cabinet Minister should stop the promotion of an Anglican on his staff who had married a Roman
Catholic and given way to the Roman rule that the children
should be baptized into her branch of the Church. The con-

siderations involved in an appointment or a promotion would, happily, rarely be of this intimate character. More often it takes the form of looking for a candidate with the right combination of connections, political, confessional, and other. There is no doubt that the confessional question is a very live one, and the situation is dominated by an inextricable mixture of politics and religion which can be paralleled, in what were once the British Isles, only in Ireland. To listen to an impassioned sermon, in a packed cathedral, telling the congregation that they were '*das Volk Christi, das Reich Christi*', with the Pope at the head, is involuntarily to recall that one had heard those words '*Volk*' and '*Reich*' resounding with an equal but different passion on ground not very remote some twenty years before, and to reflect that a priest is not precluded, even during an exposition which is textually orthodox, from invoking evil spirits.

The examples given by Eschenburg of the interests of out-side groups being brought to bear on establishments include cases involving the peasants' group and the refugees. Eschen-burg points out that the importance attributed to groups in 1945 was virtually inevitable owing to the disarray of the politi-cal parties, and he says: 'Even today there are Ministries where the key positions—not always marked as such—are occupied by high officials who in the bottom of their hearts think of them-selves more as commissars of their interest groups than as the advocate of the state. The view that certain Ministries in Federation and *Länder* are state-organized and maintained strong points in the service of the interest-groups, is fairly widely held.'[1] In a more exuberant mood Eschenburg declared that every organization would like if possible to have its own Ministry—'the doctors a health ministry, the middle class block a Ministry for the middle classes' and so on. 'All that is missing from the claims to date is a Ministry of Midwives.'[2] Claims of this nature are not unknown in other democratic countries, and are perhaps not to be avoided in the modern mass state, for which Eschenburg also has the names the 'group state' and, more comprehensively, '*der Gefälligkeitsstaat*'[3] the

[1] Eschenburg: H.d.V? p. 16.
[2] Theodor Eschenburg, *Bemerkungen zur deutschen Bürokratie* (1955), p. 12.
[3] Eschenburg: B.z.d.B., p. 18.

115

state that tries to please. One can, however, usefully distinguish between claims for the setting up of special ministries and other bodies, which are public acts and can therefore be the subject of public discussion, and the more private business of interfering with appointments and promotions inside the ministries. The latter is a truly sinister phenomenon of which this country has happily almost no experience, though there is something of the sort in the claims that are made that certain posts should be reserved for Scotsmen, Welshmen, or women.

The working of political and (through the political) of other pressures on recruitment and promotion is limited, so far as federal officials are concerned, by the operation of a government order,[1] and it would be misleading to suggest that the outside pressures play more than a subordinate—though it is by no means a negligible part—in establishments policy. The rules laid down are applicable to all officials including those of the rank of *Ministerialdirektor* (Under Secretary) and above, which, in the German system are the properly political offices whose holders have not the same security of tenure as the rest. The rules are, as is inevitable with such things, limiting rather than determining. That is to say, they lay down certain general minimal qualifications for recruitment and promotion, but cannot determine *who* is recruited or promoted. They are comparable to the conditions of eligibility for a Civil Service competition, and the choice in the hands of the particular ministry is, broadly speaking, as wide as that which, with us, is, in the matter of recruitment, open to the Civil Service Commission, though the shortage of qualified candidates has in fact meant that the freedom of choice is, at the recruitment stage, very restricted. In the matter of promotion, the British establishment officer has no regulations of any kind to guide or restrict him, though, for all but the higher posts, there are agreements with the staff which effectively govern procedure, though they leave the choice open to the authorities as in Germany.

There is little doubt, however, that the choice is not exercised in Germany in quite the same way as in England. Leaving aside the procedural differences which affect the middle and

[1] *Verordnung über die Laufbahnen der Bundesbeamten (Bundeslaufbahnverordnung— BLV)*—Bundesgesetzblatt, 8 August 1956.

lower grades only, and leaving aside the question of political influence, the German official lays greater stress than we should do on specialist knowledge, and the career of the typical administrator is made in a narrower field than is the case with us. People tend to specialize and to be promoted within the speciality. The high official faced with an awkward question feels for a specialist as Goering felt for his revolver when he heard the word 'culture'. The passion for specialization, so characteristic of the Germans and betraying their desperate hope for certainty and their basic wobbling, may increase the size but certainly cannot increase the homogeneity of the service or the facility of communications within it.

The service has, of course, already a basis for homogeneity in the academic training of the entrants. We have seen that the general administrative cadre is, in accordance with the general European pattern, an affair of lawyers, though with some who have done something less than the full course, in addition to those who have done the full course of legal studies leading up to the second state examination and others who have pursued some other supposedly utilitarian studies such as economics. There will also be a small number without university training. The academic training is never quite forgotten as it cheerfully is in England. It is recalled when people are moved from one job to another and is a factor in limiting movement. We are free of this sort of thing in our general Civil Service classes, but not outside them, where a man of fifty may still be classified as a chemist on the basis of a not very good degree he took thirty years before.

The pride in their legal training and in their specialization strengthens among German officials an *esprit de corps* which tends towards exclusiveness. It might be said that the official feels himself not only separated from the people but from his Ministers, neither of whom, he likes to think, can really appreciate the complicated laws he weaves for them. It might be said that in a blundering way the injection of political influence is an attempt to put this right. It is a blundering way, however, for it increases distrust and so makes the service a less sensitive instrument of the popular will. Only a service where there is no fear or favour, or so little as not to matter, can respond in a ready and integrated fashion to governmental control and the feeling of the country. Such steadiness is not to be found in the Germany that has known 1919, 1933 and 1945, and a bureaucracy is, after all, a secondary thing, sick or well as the country is sick or well. As to popular feeling, the German bureaucrat probably never had any antennae.

Changes of political habit in Germany would be needed if the defects of her bureaucracy were to be remedied. 'It is notable', to quote Eschenburg again, 'that the Opposition in Germany frequently restricts itself to control of the direction of policy. . . . A pre-condition of public control is not only that it succeeds in forensic criticism, but that it finds an echo in public opinion.'[1] Eschenburg is not the first German to regard his country (somewhat mistakenly one may think) as a kind of England *manqué*.

[1] Eschenburg: B.z.d.B., p. 25.

CHAPTER X

The Mind of the Administrator

A comparison of one national administration with another inevitably involves much more than a confrontation of techniques. It involves a confrontation of cultures. History pops up her head. As one walks across the courtyard of a modern prefecture certain pages of Tocqueville come to life, and as one watches the *fonctionnaire* wrestling with the evasions of his countrymen one sees Rousseau's peasant hiding his wine and his bread from the tax collector.[1] A Spanish official, whom one has met before in a gleaming modern office, suddenly appears beside one in an ancient palace. As, folded in his gown of black and crimson, he leans across the table to expound the business his sheaf of papers contains, one is faced with the deadly reasonableness of the Inquisition. These recollections have something of the fortuitous in them, but one must be deaf and blind to all tones and colours if one's gaze is not troubled by some such evocations. So sober a matter as the style of official utterances and enactments has in it something not to be accounted for in theories of organization or the science of administration, if there is one. The whole habit of French scholastic discipline, with all that is behind that, may be apparent in the text of an order or of an *Exposé des Motifs*. It is not, to say the least, obvious that British officials are writing in the language of Shakespeare until one observes that French officials are, by contrast, using the language of Racine. It is amusing to compare the 'Plain Words'[2] Gowers recommended to the British Civil Servant with 'Le Style administratif'[3] of Robert Catherine.

[1] Jean-Jacques Rousseau, *Confessions*, Livre IV.
[2] Sir Ernest Gowers: *A BC of Plain Words* (H.M.S.O.).
[3] Robert Catherine, *Le Style administratif*.

The Mind of the Administrator

The very titles indicate the difference—so characteristic of the two cultures—in the authors' points of view. For Gowers, the thing is a practical exercise. He is bent on improvement as much as any organizer of a society for the suppression of vice. He has a righteousness which he is burning to impart. For Catherine, the starting point is a simple reflection on the existence of an administrative style, leading, so appropriately for a countryman of Descartes, to 'an embryonic essay in the metaphysic'[1] of the style in question. It is only after a comparatively complicated evolution that Catherine reaches the point of putting the bias 'on the pragmatical side of the subject.' The lack of any metaphysical foreground, so to speak, almost of any spirit of pure inquiry, in the work of Gowers gives it a smugness which is, one must sadly admit, in the surest British tradition. The new righteousness is every bit as right as the old righteousness which is relegated to the dustbin. Yet, in spite of that, it is curious that Catherine, for all the superiority of his intellectual tone, succeeds in the end in seeing less of his subject than Gowers. He is almost wholly unaware that the administrative style is an instrument of government or rather, he is aware of the governmental function of the style in so far as it relates to the powers and proprieties of the hierarchy but the governed, for him, scarcely exist, whereas the constant concern of Gowers is that the words used in government should do their job which, means, in the first place, their being understood by ordinary people. It is true that Catherine is not wholly content with the French style as it is practised, and he devotes some space to '*le choix des termes*'.[2] He can underline the inelegance of a phrase, or note that an adverb may conceal an inadequacy in a thought, but it is with the complaisance of a mandarin whose empire might be crumbling unobserved before his eyes that he notes the relationship between the administrative sentence and the sentence of Proust, or observes the use of the imperfect subjunctive which tends more and more to make the official style an exception in the epistolary style of our day. This subjunctive may be said to characterize the French Civil Service as plain words do the British.

Yet in spite of national differences, there are undoubtedly

[1] Catherine, p. 10.   [2] Catherine, p. 100.

The Mind of the Administrator

important similarities to be found in the cast of mind and the outlook of administrators at home and abroad. The administrator is everywhere, and in spite of Bridges's remark about the near-artistry of his task, essentially an inartistic person. This does not mean that officials are, as a class, less sensitive in their private tastes than men of other professions. Indeed, as one migrates among the Whitehalls of Europe one has the impression that those places contain no bad samples of the civilizations of the countries they administer. It means that the administrator cannot be content with the partial and individual view of the world which, whatever general truths may be hidden in his work, are the starting points of the artist. Barrès notes in his *Journal*,[1] that he and France and Zola all had bad memories, but that each had his own peculiar memory. It was that pecularity, Zola suggested, which constituted the originality of each of the three. 'Abstractions of failing attention to the outside world,' says Ford Madox Ford 'are not necessarily in a writer signs of failing as a writer.'[2] The artist makes his work out of *his* world, a world he has invented or formerly observed. The official, on the other hand, looks as if he is claiming an impartial and general view of the world. So far from congratulating himself on having forgotten what bits of the world are like, and happily leaving them to other people to remember, he has to claim that all the facts which not he, but the world at large, think to be relevant to a particular subject, are within his grasp. By this claim he sets himself over against the individual; for many people, who have forgotten what the word used to mean, he appears to be claiming to be God. In fact the official mind, is far from opposing any kind of universality to the artist's individuality; what it does oppose to it is a kind of impersonality. The official may voluntarily exclude a large part of reality, but he does not, like the artist, do so because he can in this way give play to his personal vision of some other part. If the artist imitates nature, the official averts his eyes and makes his picture out of bits of other people's. He cannot pride himself, like Zola, on what he forgets, having to obey other people's impulses and not his own. It is characteristically the mechanical faculties, memory, logic and

[1] Maurice Barrès, *Journal*, Vol. I, p. 224.
[2] Ford Madox Ford, *Some Do Not* (1924), p. 306.

The Mind of the Administrator

the power to apprehend certain set patterns, *esprit mathématique* rather than the *esprit de finesse*, in Pascal's distinction, which are required of him. For most of his purposes an electronic brain would be better than his, but the complexity of it would be such that, whatever the progress of cybernetics, the traditional type of official is likely to remain considerably cheaper.

The official may be said not to have vision at all, except in the drabbest sense. The world he is looking at is not the same kind of world that the artist sees. Although the artist modestly admits to have forgotten much that passed outside him, the chunks he remembers and represents are solid. Even if he uses only a few lines of a pencil, or a few rhythmic words, he is concerned with something which is unmistakably whole enough to live. Things are far otherwise with the official. A whole reality is no good for the work he has to do. God might, as Berkeley says he does, hold the entire universe, with all the physical variations of its appearances, in his mind, but the official is always in search of the *relevant*. The criteria of relevance are the very definition of his job. It is here that national and in particular constitutional differences begin to appear. There is one set of criteria for the French administrator who may have one eye on his Minister and one on the *Conseil d'Etat*, and in the back of his head a calculation about the possible effects, on the policy he is advocating, of pending changes in government. There is another for the official in Bonn who, because he is singularly cut off from the administration in the *Länder*, must often have to give his advice with only a vague sense of what the detailed consequences of it will be. The head of a Swedish agency will give play to his aristocratic status as an official responsible directly to the crown as well as to his practical subordination to a democratically controlled Ministry. For the British administrator the criteria of relevance which usually appear to him in clear and compelling form, are determined by what is necessary, at a particular time, to help his Minister to ride the waves of criticism in the House, and the necessary includes what may happen at Land's End as well as what has already happened in Westminster.

The official must no doubt know more than he finally uses, in order to be satisfied that he is selecting the best for his purposes.

The Mind of the Administrator

One may say of the British official that, if he is engaged on a job with no immediate outlet to Minister and Parliament, he will still be working tacitly with the sort of notions of relevance that would mean something to them; he must try so to order things that, of all that can happen, only those things happen which are susceptible of explanation in the parliamentary context. Of the limitless number of atomic facts of which reality is made up, and out of the whole range of which the artist is free to make his pattern, only a threadbare few could possibly come into play in public discussion. The official knows so well of what kind these are that he may in time begin to think that reality is indeed constructed of them; he will call them the facts. Sometimes new kinds of interest break through into the public and parliamentary world, usually long after they have been known in the world of books, and the official may be caught off his guard, so deserving the appellation of 'hide-bound' from business men who for forty years have been thinking exclusively in terms of an even more limited range of merchandise.

The independence of the criteria of relevance employed by the official from any convictions, as distinct from habitual preconceptions, of his own, can be made out to be extremely noble or extremely ignominious. There is indeed an element of genuine self-discipline in it. The inter-connection of government, and the width of the field of public discussion in which any action of his may become embroiled, mean that he must continually be testing his logic and opinions against those of others. The luxury of the snap decision, of or the smart or good-natured bargain with the favoured customer, are not for him. Naturally, among all the situations his career will bring him into, he will encounter a wide variety of moral relationships, but his characteristic stance must be that of the man not concerned as to what is to be done, but only that what is done shall be acceptable. This can be called disinterestedness; more often it is called indifference or worse. The popular view, in other words, is rather that the official's activity is ignominious than that it is noble. Unless one takes a very optimistic view of human nature there is no occasion to quarrel with this. But if the point of the criticism is that the official is sold to a master, it is fair to inquire whether the position of his critics is in general much different, and whether something of the sort is not implied in all working for money. If one is seeking to differentiate the official from others, it is necessary to inquire for what master he works.

The notion of the ignobility of the official is implicit in Churchill's description of Sunderland: 'the zealous official, who does not care what is done so long as he is at the centre of it.'[1] It is a confrontation which is not agreeable to the official's self-esteem. It warns him of the final perils of his profession. Some German officials certainly encountered those final perils; and one cannot forget the reproach of one of them, 'that it is too much to expect heroism of everybody'. But again, the possibility of an encounter with evil is not to be removed by choosing another profession. What is peculiar in the official's position is merely that he is called upon to serve in turn masters who present themselves, as dramatically as they can, as the protagonists of opposed convictions. The tenability of the official's position rests, in the end, on the depth and nature of those convictions and the secret of their opposition. The party politician, is surely, almost as much in danger of moral distortion through being professionally bound to exaggerate differences as the official is through being professionally bound to ignore them? There is a value in the emphasis on difference, and without the dialogue between the two sides of the House the administration could not show even as much life as it does. There is, however, also a value in ignoring the differences, and the British official need not be ashamed that his profession requires him to care more for the continuity of the realm than for the success of party. Balfour had it that the Crown is above party, and the official below it. This is somewhat a *grand seigneur's* way of putting things, and it implies a rather grand notion of party to suppose that one could easily be below it. There is of course an operational sense in which Balfour's way of putting it is exact, but in the longer strategy of government the official is a dependency of party only within limits, and of the Crown, in the last analysis, without limits. That the official is a Crown servant is one of those commonplaces which, for want of active reflection upon it, many people have come to regard as a fiction, but it is indeed

[1] Winston S. Churchill, *Marlborough*, Vol. I (1933), p. 276.

the truth. For here is the official's master or, as it at present turns out, his mistress. It is no mere chance of nomenclature or technicality of the law which puts the British Civil Servant in that relationship to the Queen; it is because his task, like that of the Crown, is to maintain continuity.

The heartless character of the official is of a kind with the ultimate heartlessness of all government. One of the grand debates since the Renaissance has been on the question moved that princes may be compelled, like Machiavelli's, to all unscrupulousness to keep themselves in power. That ultimate unscrupulousness is not, however, the peculiarity of princes. It is the characteristic of all government which is determined to go on without regard to anything but survival.¹ In fact, while a puritan fastidiousness might refuse to have anything to do with government, or trade, or anything but solitude in a desert, neither Queen, politician nor official commonly face situations in which the turpitude of one course shows up grimly against the radiant goodness of a practicable alternative. No doubt such choices come unexpectedly, and Pontius Pilate was perhaps taken off his guard. The steps he took to still a particular local clamour were more or less what the service required, and he washed his hands with a civilized regret. The practice of government has its risks, but what practice has not? According to the standards of our ordinary sleepwalking, the cynicism of the official is, like that of the politician, limited by the context in which he works. The debate between the two sides of the House is far from being a debate *à l'outrance*, and although some logicians might think that a bad thing it is in fact an excellent one. For the debate in the House is as to the conditions which will or should govern the further existence of this country,

¹ In current American theory of administration, the conception of the prince whose actions are determined by his supposed need to survive has re-appeared in the context of the business world. Thus Herbert A. Simon, seeking to differentiate the objectives of the entrepreneur from those of the employee and the customer, describes them as being 'closely related to the survival of the organization' (*Administrative Behaviour*). Chester Barnard's lecture on 'Mind in Everyday Affairs', appended to *The Functions of the Executive*, compares the intellectual activities of the executive to those of a climber who, in an emergency, takes a rope between his teeth. The lecture describes illuminatingly, but with a relish which suggests an imperfect appreciation of them, the machiavellian horrors which lie at the very centre of the life of action.

The Mind of the Administrator

which would have already ceased to exist if there were no common ground in the debate. It is like a consultation between doctors, who have to decide what is best for the health of the patient but are not authorized to kill or main him. Such a consultation could become loaded with malevolence if the standard of health within the context of which they advise became distorted, as is not inconceivable. So with parliamentary government, the decisions of which are good only in so far as it works in a context of good sense. The Member of Parliament normally has to choose not between black on the one side and white on the other but between alternative ordinary mixtures of good and bad. The official works under the same broad terms of reference. He does not invent criteria of acceptability for the means he proposes; the rules of the game are that he shall take what he finds in the country at large.

'On a peu de volontés', says Rivarol, 'et c'est pourtant alors qu'on a la tête politique'.[1] It is in our sytem of government that the official should learn to discount his own opinions, and if he were thereby committed to becoming the instrument of any opinion whatever, however grotesque or barbarous, it would indeed be the case that he had become inhuman. His face would become, as Haecker noted of the faces of German generals, 'metaphysically empty'.[2] One could not say that the metaphysically empty face would seem altogether out of place in Whitehall: there have no doubt been able men who would hardly have noticed a translation to the Wilhelmstrasse. But the terms of reference in fact in this country have not become such as to demand metaphysical emptiness, and democracy, though not infallible, is not likely to demand this particular pattern. It is of course in the logic of democracy not to declare what it will in the future demand, and in so far as its terms of reference are thus unlimited it is no doubt a dangerous institution. But declared terms of reference are usually worse, because, without being able to guarantee that the good that is in them is not in the end sacrificed to the requirements of survival, they provide excuses for oppression. Nothing will guarantee a reasonable and humane environment. To those for whom the device can

[1] Antoine Rivarol, *Maximes et Pensées.*
[2] Theodor Haecker, *Tage- und Nacht-bücher* (1939–45), p. 89.

have any meaning it may seem a shift as good as any that sovereignty should rest with a Christian Queen in a Parliament less specifically committed.

It is the absolute nonentity of the British administrator that is his chief merit. Without making extravagant claims one may safely suggest that as much practical ability is collected in the acres around Whitehall as in any comparable area elsewhere in the world, but it is, to revert to Gambetta's phrase, if not quite in the sense in which he intended it, the ability of *quelque chose* rather than of *quelqu'un*. That is not to say that the ordinary human foibles, what is called force of character and the various colours of personality, are not to be found there as elsewhere. But the enterprise is in its nature impersonal because it is constitutionally subordinate, and it is in its constitutional subordination, completed by an utter lack of pretence to arcane qualifications, that its characteristic merit lies. It is true that the British administrator, like indeed the administrator everywhere, is suspected rather of being insubordinate and of being rather full of *volontés* than otherwise. To the suspicion naturally attaching to people whose work is done near the centres of power, there has been added since the days of Max Weber, and *a fortiori* since the days of James Burnham, a suspicion, of a rather more shadowy kind, that historical forces are somehow working to put power in the hands of the bureaucrats and managers in general. Burnham was, however, not particularly brilliant as a judge of historical forces. Writing about 1940 (his book was copyrighted in the United States in 1941) he boldly stated that 'the localization of sovereignty in parliament is ended save for a lingering remnant,' and that in England it might 'not last the next few months'.[1]

The Managerial Revolution may be regarded as a vulgarization of Max Weber, and in defence of that it could have been said, to be sure, that if ever a man needed a little vulgarization Max Weber did. It was intended as a philosophy of revolution, the revolutionary element consisting of a large injection of Karl Marx and a tone of menacing prophecy, accompanied, of course, by an assumption of scientific objectivity which is forgivable since it was accompanied by a confession that, in general,

[1] James Burnham, *The Managerial Revolution* (London, 1942), p. 141.

The Mind of the Administrator

'the sociological and historical sciences have not yet reached even the level that the physical sciences held in ancient Greece'.[1] Burnham supposed 'that the conclusions reached' in his book would be 'displeasing to most of those who read it'.[2] Perhaps this was a joke or a manifestation of the author's flair for publicity, for Burnham's own theory must have told him that a large public of managers was in fact waiting to be told how important they were. Some of them, it is true, might not like the crude simplifications as to the nature of society, but it was obvious that a sufficient number of people would raven down the theory with the flattery. What Burnham in fact had concocted was a sort of opium for the managerial middle classes. The people his theory reassures are 'production managers, operating executives, superintendents, administrative engineers, supervisory technicians; or, in government (for they are to be found in governmental enterprise just as in private enterprise) . . . administrators, commissioners, bureau heads, and so on . . . these who already for the most part in contemporary society are actually managing, on its technical side, the actual process of production, no matter what the legal and financial form— individual, corporate, governmental—of the process.'[3] These people were not those engaged in tasks 'which need elaborate training in the physical sciences and in engineering', but those engaged in 'direction and co-ordination'. They might, however, sometimes have to have 'an acquaintance with the physical sciences or the psychological and social sciences since human beings are not the least among the instruments of production'.[4]

Burnham understands by a ruling class 'a group of persons who, by virtue of special social-economic relations, exercises a special degree of control over access to the instruments of production and receives preferential treatment in the distribution of the product of these instruments'. The question of who rules in that marxist sense is of somewhat limited interest. On this view of the matter, the fact that what a man achieves has no relationship to what he aims at does not matter. In the classic case, he fights for freedom of conscience and wakes up, it is alleged, with political power. This comedy will no doubt continue to be played as long as there are human beings with

[1] Burnham, p. 261.   [2] Burnham, p. 259.   [3] Burnham, p. 76.   [4] Burnham, p. 75.

128

mixed motives and muddled heads, but the deluded victor cuts a poor figure as a ruler. He may indeed be the man who has permission to eat most, but when one has taken a bored look at this prodigy one is still left with the question as to who, if anybody, rules in the sense of understanding what is happening and, with a full sense of the limitations of effective action, being able at an appropriate moment to give a directing touch. Whether or not the administrators with whom this book has been concerned count as 'managers' in Burnham's sense—and it would seem that he would clearly regard them as one with the commissioners and bureau heads—they undoubtedly appear to some people as a ruling class in this other sense. It is the fear that they are, that the official may originate something—naturally something unpleasant—and by virtue of his position impose it on the rest of society, which leads people to try to control him in a legal straight-jacket and to inject a little more political influence under his skin. The remedies are superficial but the anxieties they are meant to cure are deep. Notions of what is meant by originating something differ not a little.

The British official is undoubtedly a powerful person in the sense that he occupies an influential place in the system of our government and that his advice is always listened to and generally taken; and 'power', says Professor Beer, means 'the ability of someone to get his decisions accepted by others'.[1] No doubt if the person making the 'decision' were in fact in a position to decide what he liked you would have there a definition of absolute power. The American professor, however, was writing about the British Treasury, and it is certainly not the case that Treasury or any other officials in Britain can get accepted by the government or the country at large any decision they care to make. The context is so powerful as to be almost everything. Government is by opinion, and the official's power is limited by the necessity he is under of accepting the opinions as well as the facts of the day. Indeed, it may be said that the extent to which an official feels that he is exercising real power is a measure of his lack of originality or even of individual perception, at the very least of his contentment with the preconceptions of the age. The official is a kind of second-hand

[1] S. H. Beer, *Treasury Control* (1956), p. 107.

merchant; the only ideas of direct use to him are those that are vulgar and current. He may be thought of as a walking '*Dictionnaire des Idées Reçues*' or, at the most daring, of ideas which are receivable by the world at large. To be brilliant, he has to be one move ahead of Bouvard and Pécuchet, but only one move. If the real powers in a society are those who get their ideas accepted by others, he is in no better case than the bus conductor or the barber, and his not inconsiderable wisdom, like theirs, comes from having had to listen to so many clients.

The official is of course not ordinarily conscious of the restrictions of his habits of thought, any more than is the member of a primitive tribe who none the less seems to the visiting anthropologist generally to be pounding around a narrow circle. Moreover, Whitehall like the primitive tribe is an ordinary human society, in which accordingly almost anything can happen. The official assuredly does not feel tongue-tied, and the discussions that go on in these offices certainly show no unusual degree of respect for successful personages or received ideas. Indeed it might rather be said that the constant preoccupation with other people's ideas and importances produces an attitude of scepticism and irony, which is prevented from becoming dominant only by the constant and imperative need for action which must be in terms of publicly acceptable ideas. The relations between Ministers and Permanent Secretary, or of the member of a commission or committee with the principal who acts as its secretary, are not restricted by the constitutional limits. The decision, or the recommendation, is unequivocally the responsibility of the Minister or the committee, but all manner of things may have been said by the officials before they are arrived at. Clearly it is desirable that Ministers, and chairmen and members of committees, should be people both patient to listen to advice and firm in drawing their own conclusions. It is, however, also desirable that the officials nearest to them should be, not merely well-informed on the subject in hand but intelligent and willing to speak their minds. At any rate it is difficult to see any advantage to the public in these people being either stupid or timid, and no Minister or committee member worth his salt will be intimidated by some marks of ability. Of course those for whom any advice is bad if it come from an official are appalled at the risk that the political decision may be more exclusively the work of an official than it should be, and it is no part of the thesis of this book to pretend that the official should have his way against the proper authorities. On the other hand it can hardly be contended that it is a very great evil that the advice of officials who, by the nature of their job, are likely at least to be acquainted with the pitfalls surrounding a particular decision, should play a part in the making of that decision. The advice the official gives, if he finds even too ready a listener, is very unlikely to be merely a good idea of his own. He will have had too much experience of affairs to believe that an individual good idea is of much value in action. His error is more likely to be relying too heavily on what Bridges calls the 'departmental philosophy', which is nothing else than the resultant of previous experience in the field in question.

The administrator is likely to remain sceptical of any general theory as to the source of the ideas which in the end determine his action. They seem to him to come from here and there, from one corner of the kingdom or another, from one group or organization or another. He deals with them as rising forces and not as ideas. If this holding the ring is ruling, no doubt he has a hand in it. If to rule is to generate the ideas, the vulgarizations of which turn the course of history, no doubt Shelley is in the right of it, and the rulers are not men in Whitehall, or even men who badger Whitehall but people who stay at home writing surprising sentences or drawing unexpected lines on paper.

CHAPTER XI

Reforms and Imitations

It is a common and proper ambition to wish to reform the Civil Service, and it is impossible to look at certain features of continental practice without wondering whether our own administration could be improved by adopting them. No one is likely to suggest the introduction of civil governors or prefects as general supervisors in the provinces on behalf of the central power. The conception is too far outside our traditions and habits of thought. Such an official would certainly not arouse here any admiration for his 'touch of authority', rather a general and effective murmur of 'Who does he think he is?' If further regional co-ordination were needed, it would come by an unobtrusive development of the regional organization of ministries, which have already, and sufficiently unobtrusively, aligned their regional boundaries with one another. Some of the other characteristic features of continental systems are more seductive. It may be said that, by general European standards (1) the education of our administrators is inadequate and their training slipshod; (2) our administrators show a lack of appreciation of law; and (3) they are too reluctant to take public and political responsibility.

(1) First, as to education and training. What is in effect suggested is that a man who is to be an administrator should first study administration. Either before he enters the service, or in his early years in it, he should acquire a body of academic knowledge useful to him in his profession. The knowledge that comes by experience of business is supposed not to be enough. This was Taylor's view in 1836; it is, evidently, the general European view at the present time.

The field of administrative studies is singularly ill-defined;

Reforms and Imitations

it is by no means certain that it is susceptible of precise definition. It is tempting to believe, with Gladden, that there is in
fact a body of knowledge which will enable the student to
'approach a new project as an expert who knows most of the
answers'.[1] But where is it to be found? There are descriptive
works which tell you the structure of governments and of administrative organizations; there are—particularly in America
—manuals which define 'organization', 'decision', and 'co-
operation' and contain stirring stuff about the heroism of 'executives'; there are—again mainly in America—case studies in
business and public administration, sometimes written up as
a sort of administrative science fiction.[2] Whatever the merits of
these classes of work, none of them, certainly, will give the
expertise Gladden seems to promise. Perhaps Gladden has in
mind rather that the administrator should study, not administration as such (whatever, in the abstract, that may be) but the
subject matter of his future work. Even in that case his words
bespeak not only a vain hope but a dangerous misconception.
The administrator is not a schoolmaster, and neither people nor
politicians want him to be. He does not, characteristically, know
and instruct; if he is wanted at all, it is as an instrument of wills
other than his own. This does not mean that his function is to
shout a hurried 'Yes, sir' to every ejaculation of a hydra-
headed public or of a government which only an elaborate
administrative organization can prevent from being itself hydra-
headed. On the contrary, he will with his colleagues often act
as a resistance to weaken or delay an impulse, though sometimes
he may conduct it to an unexpectedly quick and full execution.
But the speed and nature of his reaction are not a function of a
studious expertise. The administrator is part of an elaborate
system of connections, and his service to public and politicians
should be to ensure the orderliness of the impulses transmitted
to the system. Of course in one sense he *knows* quite a lot, but
what he knows is not stuff that can be learned academically. It
is rather the rules of the possible in a particular place and time,
and in a particular subject matter. This knowledge he has as the
man who happens to be sitting in a particular office at that stage
of the business, responsible for the running of a particular

[1] See above, p. 35.   [2] See above, p. 41.

machine and with a ready set of connections to Minister and Parliament and those parts of the public to whom the matters he is handling are of importance. So far from knowing most of the answers beforehand, he has scrupulously to ascertain what, at a particular time and place, the answer could be. Experts outside will assure him that they know what is best. There will be different bests; but the solution will have to be a single possible.

It may be argued that although previous studies in a particular field cannot tell a man the answers, in a particular time and place, to the question 'What is to be *done*?' and although such answers can only be given from the point in the administrative system where the pressures and advices of those concerned meet, yet the man who has had previous specialist training will be better able to seize the significance of these pressures and advices. According to this view, an entrant into the Administrative Class might be precluded from entering the Ministry of Health unless he had spent his undergraduate years studying the hospital system or from entering the Ministry of Labour unless he had spent them studying the structure and working of Trade Unions. There are not lacking, in the universities, people willing to give instruction in the working of any bit of national or nationalized organisation. The mere removal of a problem from the great world into the cover of a university does not, however, mean that the pressures impinging on the solutions offered have been removed. On the contrary, one is removing it from a milieu where all the pressures which have to be taken account of should be felt to one where selected and sometimes irrelevant pressures are at work. Will the recruit be better for having been exposed to these partial dogmatisms, or partial scepticisms? The official of the Ministry of Health will have to learn something about hospitals, the official of the Ministry of Labour will have to learn something about Trades Unions, but are these things, for the purposes of the job he has to do, better learned at the hands of the outside student or by an apprenticeship in which he will see how the views of professors go into the melting pot with an almost infinite variety of other pressures and opinions to make a viable government decision?

The training of administrators fitted only for work in a particular field is perhaps not often advocated, though the teaching of certain specialist subjects seems to imply such advocacy and may in time create a lobby in support of such notions. In our system, it would, even if it were thought to be profitable for limited ends, be open to the objection that it would abolish the laicity and break the unity of the central administration, and before these are tampered with it would be well to reflect on the connection of these characteristics with parliamentary control and with the coherence of the realm.

What is studied by the aspirant to a career in public administration, in those countries which demand an elaborate preliminary training, is in the main neither the general science of administration (if such a thing exists outside American text-books) nor the subject-matter of his future work, as such, but the law, supplemented, to a greater or less degree, by economic and social studies which may, certainly, be regarded as a sort of introduction to possible future subject-matters. The most valuable part of the training given by the *Ecole Nationale d'Administration* is, however, almost certainly, not the theoretical studies at the school but the experience of administration at the prefecture. The value of this experience is that it acquaints the student with some of the characteristics of the milieu in which he is to work. Theoretical studies of administrative subjects, in all countries, really have the same objective. They are everywhere strongly marked by the local and historical characteristics of the country. Some of the American manuals of administration are so many sparks thrown off by vast capitalist enterprises as they hurtle onwards; in this world thought is secondary to action and action to mere propulsion. A book like the manual of administration by Hans Peters,[1] even while it attempts to get away from the traditional German obsession with the legal aspects of administration, staggers to the subject through a Teutoburger Forest of Germanic abstractions about the Idea of the State. The administrative law which is the basis of most continental training is a national, even a provincial matter. These studies may give some sort of acquaintance with the milieu in which the future administrator is to work. They can do no more, and their prevalence is certainly no decisive

[1] Hans Peters, *Lehrbuch der Verwaltung.*

135

argument against the British system which favours apprenticeship by way of travel from job to job rather than the reading of
Baedeker in advance for a diploma.

There is a certain measure of absolute foolishness about, for
example, some of the conceptions of American theorists and
a certain degree of objective pedantry about some of the continental reliance on administrative law as a means of induction
to the public service. An important reason for the appearance of
grotesqueness in these manuals and methods is, however, the
irrelevance of some of their most characteristic features to the
milieu in which the British official has to work. This is particularly true of the continental system. We may not be able to
assert that we have no administrative law, but there is still a
marked difference between its nature and place with us and its
nature and place in countries where the state is conceived of as
a complex of legal relationships. This difference is likely to
persist as long as we are spared the horrors of a revolutionary
break and foreign domination. There could therefore be no
question of applying directly to the training of British Civil
Servants the methods employed in France or Germany, nor
are the minds of young men likely to be improved by spending
their undergraduate days with the books produced by American
schools of administration. What the British administrator needs,
to fulfil his constitutional rôle, is a mind open to the point of
agnosticism as to the solutions which may be applied to the
problems he has to deal with, and a resolution sensitive to the
conditions in which viable decisions can be made. The latter is
a temper he must acquire in the course of miscellaneous and
often tiresome work, between Ministers and Parliament on one
side and the population at large on the other. The former is to
be produced, if at all, by a liberal education, and there may
certainly be those who doubt whether a general liberality in
education is any longer possible.

It would be amusing to set out a new scheme of liberal education which might be supposed to produce minds sufficiently
open and sufficiently trained to understand the trickles of thought
behind the streams of opinion which determine political action.
It would be possible to maintain that the requisite degree of
understanding of what is going on in this country could only

be found in young men who had read the *Tractatus Logico-Philosophicus*[1] and *The Shape of the Liturgy*[2] as well as say, the *Republic* and the essays of Montaigne. One could elaborate a programme made up, like the literary programmes propounded by Ezra Pound, of all the things one had the impression of having sharpened one's wits on, or like the dreams of ambitious fathers, of all the things one had through lethargy or lack of opportunity missed. But a government service cannot afford these idiosyncrasies. Nothing has happened to alter the conception that you should accept the current standard of what constitutes a good general education and take your candidates from among those who have received such an education. If a progressive fragmentation of learning has made the conception of a general liberality a more difficult or disputed one, that is something to be worked out by those whose profession it is to think and not by the Civil Service Commission whose function, like that of the service itself, is to act on current conceptions rather than to set up as an inventor of new ones. What can be asserted, from a merely practical and even political point of view, is that the survival of some kind of liberal and general education, and of administrators who are not daunted by specialities but take it for granted that the practical implications of all of them can be explored and explained by a sufficiently agile lay mind, is indispensable to the survival of parliamentary government or indeed of any goverment based on free discussion.

So far as the foreign notions of what can be done for the instruction of future administrators differ from our merely liberal pattern it is due to constitutional and general conditions which differ from our own. It does not appear anywhere to have been demonstrated that recruits to public administration must be in possession of a certain body of knowledge, as the specialist must, but they have certainly, before they can be effective, to be assimilated by the corps they are joining. The *Ecole Nationale d'Administration* combines the functions of training and recruitment; to an outsider, it seems to be of more significance as the maw and digestion of the higher French Civil Service than as an instructor. The Treasury's modest scheme of training for

[1] Ludwig Wittgenstein.   [2] Gregory Dix.

137

Assistant Principals has no other object than to assist in the assimilation of these newcomers to the service.

(2) The charge that British administrators do not show a proper appreciation of law is in its nature more difficult to deal with than the charge that they are inadequately trained. One is at once involved in constitutional and even more deep-seated national differences. 'For we have in France', said Montaigne— long before 1789—'more laws than all the rest of the world put together, and more than would be needed to regulate all the worlds of Epicurus. . . . What have our legislators gained by selecting a hundred thousand particular facts and cases, and attaching a hundred thousand laws to them? This number bears no relation to the infinite diversity of human actions. The multiplication of our inventions will never attain to the full variety of what really happens.' Montaigne had seen the laws in use in the Parlement of Bordeaux. 'Who has seen children trying to divide up a lump of quicksilver into a definite number of parts: the more they press and mould it and try to force it to obey their law, the more they irritate the liberty of this generous metal.' So the affairs of men elude the refinements of the legislator, and endless argument and interpretation 'dissipate the truth and destroy it'.[1] The essay is entitled *De l'Expérience.* In another essay Montaigne says 'that it would be better to make the laws will what they can achieve since they cannot achieve what they will'.[2] It is a counsel we are far from having always followed, though we have followed it more closely than Montaigne's own land of France. It is, certainly, the golden maxim for the administrator. He is concerned with the possible, and whether he is preparing a new law or supervising the execution of an existing one he must look through the law to the realities it is supposed to seize. And because sometimes it will not seize them, he must have a little of the quality for which Plutarch praised Philopœmen, that 'being born to command, he knew not only now to command according to the law, but could command the law itself upon necessity, and when the commonwealth required it'.[3] He must

---

[1] Montaigne, *Essais,* Livre III, chap. XIII.   [2] Montaigne, Livre I, chap. XXIII.
[3] *Plutarch's Lives,* English version of Sir Thomas North, 'The Comparison of Titus Quintius Flamininus with Philopœmen'.

be on the look-out for failures to achieve the ends designed by Parliament, and suggest to his Minister amendments that would make the law fit more closely to reality.

For the administrator the law is an instrument. It is one of a number, not always the best. sometimes quite unuseable. No doubt without experience of work which is, in the strict sense, administration of the law, no one can pretend, in Whitehall, to be even tolerably seasoned. But there is, evidently, a great deal of work, among it some of the most basic and important, which does not involve the administration of the law at all. Even where the work is of this character, the law is, for the administrator, no more than one of the limiting conditions in which his work has to be done. It defines the terms of reference for his action in a particular field. The work that can be done is, however, limited by a number of other conditions which are not less significant for the practical effect of his action. These include the policy of the government and the temper of Parliament, and the economic conditions of the day which will already have played a rôle in forming the political conditions. They will also include technical administrative conditions, which may be affected by the quality of the staff it is possible to employ. A statute book crammed with lovely things is pointless without the means to carry them into practice. Indeed it is a sign of a softening of the brain to tolerate such a state of affairs. It is an excellent practice to test out a field for possible legislation by seeking to encourage voluntary agreement and action within it, and to legislate only when, by the measure of what has in this way been done, it is possible to judge the practicability and usefulness of the legislation proposed, and it is not the least of the merits of this proceeding that it may sometimes demonstrate that there is no need for legislation at all.

Legislation which places duties, rights or mere restrictions on the citizen should of course do so in the most unequivocal terms of which the subject is susceptible. The citizen should know where he is and the courts be in a position to declare invalid what is not in accordance with the declared will of parliament. Those fine principles are nowhere in dispute, but, as with the law itself, the difficulties occur in its application. The multifarious nature of reality was not a dream of Montaigne's study.

139

Reforms and Imitations

The man did not dream; he perceived. There is no possibility of laws which are clear beyond question for all the extraordinary cases which can arise, and the citizen cannot in such cases know in advance precisely where he stands. That is his greatest need, and the courts can ensure it no more than the administration. The court's decision is uncertain and may seem whimsical. It is at least as likely to disconcert the citizen as the decision of the administration. There is no particular merit in going to the courts every time the case is not unarguably clear. The unwieldiness of legal procedures makes them more suitable for great cases than for small. No doubt there is an immutable justice, but those who argue in wigs and gowns have no magical access to it. The outcome of a case in court may turn more on a matter of legal construction than on any question of substance of interest to the citizen who appeals, and the services of the judges to the community may be as much to the refinement of the literary style of the enactments as to the direct benefit of the individual. Let no one belittle this exalted literary criticism; it has its uses, though it can serve to bedevil and confuse the citizen as well as to protect him. The *conseiller* at the Parlement of Bordeaux had something to say on this subject too. What matters to the citizen in doubt about his position under any enactment is that he should come finally to an authority he feels to be fair by the standards of the day, and which other people in like case, who have taken the decision of the administration without question, feel will not unduly favour him. The judges will in many cases do as much; they can in no case do more. They may in some matters, such as the question of what constitutes obscenity in literature, move more slowly with the changes of opinion than would an authority more directly dependent on Parliament, but that is not necessarily a bad thing. The basic question is one of confidence in the authorities and the citizen's sense of freedom. The power of government is vast and intrusive, and it is essential that it should be possible publicly to question any one of its actions. But let no one pretend that, in this matter, the rôle of the courts is what it was when Charles I was ruling without a parliament. The parts played by parliament and courts in the service of individual liberty are complementary; and in our day the part of the former is overwhelmingly predominant.

Parliaments—though not ours—have been known to vote away the fundamental liberties of the subject and there is no supernatural security in this or in any other human institution. The British administrator who allows himself a predilection for the liberties of the country he serves will be glad that they do not hang by any one thread, in Parliament or elsewhere. If he thinks some legal criticisms of the administration inept, he will certainly not wish for any diminution of the prestige and independence of the courts, and he may reflect that such incomprehension of the practice of government as was shown by Hewart's book is in the end more likely to discredit the judicature than the executive.

It is not to be taken as evidence of lack of appreciation of the law by the administrator if he does not adopt a lawyer's point of view. The lawyer may properly examine the doings of the administration and seek to apply to them the principles which have secured the rule of law in this country. The administrator, however, has his own legitimate point of view. His task, carried out in a context in which he is constitutionally subordinate, is nothing less than the care of all that makes the polity survive, and he is entitled to criticize, from this point of view, legal procedures which threaten the efficient execution of the tasks entrusted to his Minister by Parliament. One may reflect with profit on Jolowicz's comment on the Byzantine attempt 'to forbid by legislation evils which could only have been overcome, if at all, by a far-seeing economic policy'.[1] To pretend that the administrator can be reduced to a bit of legal mechanism, with all his duties written down, is nonsense. He holds a long conversation with the citizen, with politicians, and with his colleagues, and on the quality of that conversation the quality of government largely depends. For him the law has no finality; he is for ever, under proper authority, revising and remaking it. For him it represents not a deposit of sacred wisdom but a record of stages reached in the conversation, of pronouncements made and engagements taken, for a time.

[1] Jolowicz, p. 521.

141

(3) As to the charge that British administrators are too reluctant to take public and political responsibility, the main modifications of the present system which a comparison with continental methods might suggest would be a greater openness as to the advice administrators give, and the identification of senior officials with the aims of politicians. The former change might be achieved by something like the access to public documents which is supposed to be practised in Sweden, so that the part played by each official could be publicly known; the latter by giving a special semi-political status and a less secure tenure to certain senior officials and by allowing Ministers to bring a number of politically committed assistants with them into their Departments. Neither of these changes would be mere administrative changes. The former would amount to a violence to the constitution, for it would make of the administrator a man who mattered, competing in his own right for public attention and support, instead of his being, as he is at present, the mere servant of a Minister of the Crown. Although it may have a few academic supporters in this country it is never likely to be advocated by politicians with experience of office. It would not, in its consequences, be tolerated by the public, who expect to be able to bring responsibility for the doings of the Civil Service home to their elected representatives. And anyway, as we have seen, it does not in fact work in Sweden in the way its apologists suppose. The second suggestion, involving a certain politicization of the administration, is less patently absurd, but its consequences would be scarcely less nefarious. It is to be noted that although not technically incompatible with the doctrine of Ministerial responsibility, the suggestion implies that that doctrine is played out and that Ministers can no longer pretend to answer in Parliament for what their Departments are up to.

It is certainly true that government and parliament can attend to only a fraction of the business which has to be done to keep the polity going. It is, however, absurd to suggest that because the political head of a Ministry does not do all the work himself he cannot be in control of it. One could take any other point in the system and assert for example that the assistant secretary or the principal, or the senior executive officer were not in control of the divisions of the work they are supposed to be responsible for. Evidently any organization, in the government service or outside it, can be so unwieldy that the nominal head has a less clear view of its working than he should, but that is not a general criticism of the Whitehall system but a warning that the system of transmission must be kept under continuous scrutiny. It is to be suspected that some who complain that Ministers have less power over their departments than they should have not reflected sufficiently on what Ministers are in fact constitutionally empowered to do. A politician who takes over a Ministry is far from being thereby given authority to do what he likes with it. The bulk of the Department's work is likely to consist of the administration of laws which former Parliaments have put on the statute book, and unless and until he gets authority for revision the new Minister is as much bound by them as any official or any other citizen. Moreover, it is nobody's wish that a new Minister should, even within the law, act without regard to what passed before he took over, or that the reasonable expectations of the people with whom his officials have been dealing should be left out of account. The Minister, in other words, enters when he takes office into a system of legal, institutional and personal relationships of great complexity and he can start his work only from affairs as he finds them. The capable Minister can make his impression; there is no question about that. If the less capable finds it more difficult, that is surely not altogether a bad thing; or if it is thought intolerable that such a Minister should feel himself thwarted by officials the remedy should not be to give Ministers feebler advisers.

Those who think that the political impulsions in the machine are in fact not strong enough are certainly in the right when they suggest, as they are apt to do, that a Minister cannot exercise the supervision in detail of the affairs of his office that he could in the days of Taylor's 'Statesman'. A perusal of the files of even twenty or thirty years ago will show that even so recently many matters were brought to the personal attention of Ministers which would now be dealt with by officials not of the highest ranks. It would be foolish to assert that nothing had been lost in quality of work in the great expansion of the government service which has taken place, though there have been gains as well as losses, and it is by no means certain that any of the weaknesses of the system are attributable to a deficiency of political impulse. The methods of increasing the political voltage of government departments which have been employed on the continent can hardly be said to promise any increase of administrative efficiency, whatever merits in principle they may be supposed to have. Some of the most senior and influential posts in departments would be turned into political appointments. The men who filled them might still in general be men who had made their careers in the public service, but they would be known to be of the same political colour as their Ministers and would look for their future careers to the political success of their masters. We should have a form of spoils system. The argument for this system is that permanent officials cannot be trusted to share the enthusiasm of politicians and that they will be less effective advisers and executants than men who share in the Ministers' political convictions and ambitions. This view is rarely held by the politician who has had experience of office, who may have found his wily Permanent Secretary no bad guide through the complexities that had to be come to terms with before new policies could be made effective, and who will certainly have found in all his senior officials the ingrained habit of doing their best to help their Minister to avoid, or at least to be able to meet, Parliamentary criticism. However that may be, it is to be noted that our system requires a man who takes ministerial office to find out what he is about and to be able to stand up in the House and answer for what is being done in his name. His ultimate isolation is as much part of the system as his ultimate loss of identity in the collective decisions of the cabinet. It may encourage a Minister's predilections if he is able to make himself cosy in his Ministry with people who can be relied upon to share them, but it is difficult to see how it would increase his understanding of the problems he has to answer for.

Under our present system the Minister generally has one or more political assistants in the Department—the Parliamentary Secretaries. The Parliamentary Secretary does not, however, provide the kind of additional political propulsion the admirers of continental ways would like to see introduced into our system. He is by way of being an assistant to his Minister, who will delegate to him certain functions, in the House and in the office. In the typical case the Parliamentary Secretary is an able young man who is learning about the conduct of business and may hope, if he does well, to be promoted in time to a senior ministerial post. He is, so to speak, outside the main line of command and does not in any sense come between the Minister and the Department, for which the Minister is solely responsible. What the reformers dream of is to introduce into ministries people who will get under the skin of the officials, though what they would hope to find under that tegument is a mystery. However politely the case is put, it amounts, of course, to an expression of lack of confidence in officials, and a belief that the politician is by nature more trustworthy. There might be something to be said for a society run entirely by politicians, but one might as well dream of a society of nymphs and shepherds. In our complicated society there are and are going to be a lot of officials, and the only question is whether anything is to be gained by making within their ranks a distinction between those the Minister has to put up with and those he can really trust. It need hardly be said that such a distinction would cause a decline of confidence as between Ministers and officials, and would produce serious faults in transmission within the service. There is little doubt that the continental devices operate in this way, and it is indeed extraordinary that in this country, which long ago got rid of political patronage in the service, anyone should be found to wish to re-introduce those evils. We may be a little peculiar in having a wholly independent service with the habit of professional indifference to party politics but that hardly seems reason enough for getting rid of it. And if the introduction of politically-minded officials in the immediate neighbourhood of the Minister had little to recommend it, their introduction at any other point in the system would no doubt be administratively worse. There is little doubt that the French prefectoral system is effective in the measure—and it is a very large measure —in which the prefects have found means of counteracting the effects of their political dependency. A system which invites political intervention at various points in the administrative structure must diminish the sense of responsibility to the

Minister at the top and so, indeed, imperil the unity, evenness and fairness of the administration.

The desire to politicize the administration is the most malignant form of common aspiration to render it more *human*. Various and diverse intentions are hidden under this aspiration. The Nazis certainly considered that they were infusing life into a dead system when they put their placemen and spies into the German bureaucracy. The whole thing was going to throb in unison with the great German heart, the pulse of which was at the time rather marked. With us the intention is the more harmless one of infusing a bland democratic sentiment everywhere, sometimes merely of persuading bureaucrats to behave like real people, which they are supposed not to do. It is incontrovertible, however, that even the most extensive bureaucracies are staffed by human creatures, who can hardly help behaving as such, and there seems to be no point in trying to make a merit out of that. No doubt it is desirable that they should be as reasonable as possible, and polite in accordance with the standards of the age. Any special determination to give evidence of humanity might quickly pall, like the courtesy of air hostesses. At worst, it might deteriorate into misplaced initiatives or corruption, which latter we should remember is a human norm. There is a tendency for all administrative units to turn into little, extremely human, societies which serve for the benefits of their members rather than for anyone else's, and this is one of the problems even of decentralizations uncomplicated by political interventions. The characteristic of the efficient adminstrative machine is not any over-weaning humanity in its inmates but rather their discipline and impersonality.

A government department is a collection of people, but if they are to do their work effectively they must try so far as possible collectively to resemble a *thing*. It is a simplification, but one which contains the essence of the matter, to say that the department is an apparatus for the transmission of impulses from government to people and from people to government. The former is the accepted executive function, but without the latter connection a modern government would be quite unable to do its work. The politicians of course have their own system of connections with the population at large, but for the planning of particular tasks, for the mere enforcement of existing legislation, special systems of wills and forces have to be ascertained and understood in relation to other wills and forces. Anything which impedes the two-way flow between government and population may be said to be an administrative flaw, and it is in the light of this, and not of preconceptions about the superior vigour or clarity of vision of the man with political commitments, that questions of organization should be considered.

It is not too much to say that there are no *direct* lessons to be learned from European practice in administration. The Swedish law on the publication of official documents, or the Austrian law of administrative procedure, for example, are not mere devices that could be used anywhere to produce the beneficial effects which they undoubtedly produce in their proper constitutional context. They are essentially not solutions to administrative problems—if indeed such things as purely administrative problems may be said to exist at all—but responses, more or less slow, coming from sources more or less deep in the histories of the countries concerned, to particular political problems of a more or less enduring sort. The British system of administration, like any other, is always in need of reform, and is in some measure always being reformed. Now and then some more radical change is needed than that represented by mere internal adaptation, but even such major changes cannot well be made by bringing in bits of institutions from outside Britain; they can hardly be otherwise than by modification of the system we have in response to changes in the country itself.

The habits of the British administration are merely aspects of the national political habit, of the general cast of mind that history and languages have produced. 'For dullness, the creeping Saxon' was a phrase Matthew Arnold had pleasure in quoting[1] when he was making use of the Welsh bards to give colour to his excellent denunciations of his fellow-countrymen. The phrase is exact. A Frenchman put it that he greatly appreciated the talent the English had for remaining silent in company without there being any embarrassed feeling that something should be said. The talents of the nation are not discursive, which is why

[1] Matthew Arnold, *The Study of Celtic Literature* (1867), p. 99.

we, in our turn, greatly appreciate the discourse of France. But dullness and the capacity to wait are not bad qualifications for practical affairs. It is a vulgar error to suppose that whoever ceases to discourse ceases to think—and a worse one to suppose that the mere grinding out of logical discourse is necessarily a sign of anything that is really worth calling thought. It is not unintelligent to proceed tentatively, like a cat, smelling and looking hard at all the relevant information before you decide which way to jump. A reluctance to be explicit on all occasions does not necessarily imply a contempt for the clarities of reason. That the British Constitution works, that a considerable people have been able to live under it with their various opinions and develop and change their economic and social life, is rightly judged to be a more important thing than any theoretical statement that can be made about it, and it is not unreasonable for people brought up under it not to be vividly impressed by the fine principles in the constitutions of say, the First, Second, Third or Fourth French Republics or in the American Declaration of Independence. No doubt if we were starting from scratch we should have to have some such stuff but, more through luck than judgment, we have hitherto avoided the disasters which would make that necessary. And so it is not necessary.

However strong one's native conviction that foreigners are queer a glance at Europe makes it plain that it is we who are odd. Constitution-making, and the passion for legal precisions and codifications which go with it, are normal in the western world and these habits of mind have indeed been among the most popular of western exports to other parts of the world. This is not, however, absolute proof of the idealism and intelligence of the rest of the world and of our own sub-humanity. Constitution-making is normal because defeat and revolution are normal. That British history has been a little odd in this matter is not a thing we should ourselves take much credit for; on the other hand, it is not in itself proof of our political incapacity and the traces and consequences in our administrative behaviour of a long period of domestic peace, though they give that behaviour a singularity, do not suggest that it should be remodelled on the pattern of less fortunate lands. It is a basic fallacy in comparative studies to suppose that

148

Reforms and Imitations

whoever is in a minority, even of one, is necessarily wrong. On the other hand, it is not to be denied that the requirements of international negotiation and—what is sometimes much the same thing—of international publicity, make it necessary to approximate, at any rate superficially, to foreign habits. The Atlantic Charter was a most un-English document. It might be said to have derived from the French revolutionary streak in the American tradition and it was addressed to what the signatories hoped was a revolutionary situation. The voluminous codifications which international bodies in general love to produce tend to be more in the spirit of Latin legislation than of our own. These are games we have to play if we are not to be left out in the cold.

The pressure put on us to be more like other people is such that one may wonder how long our remaining insularities will survive. As long ago as 1912 Georges Sorel announced that England was 'beginning to be like other countries'.[1] He did not think he was foretelling a great happiness for us. On the contrary, he was foretelling our senescence and disorder. We still have a certain singularity, however. There is no point in speculating how much of what remains is irreducible. Above all there is no point in defending singularity as such. The only idiosyncrasy worth having, in a person or a nation, is what cannot be got rid of by the ordinary social process of rubbing shoulders with other people or with other nations. One should not pride oneself on oddity, nor on the other hand should one set out to copy other people from a notion that other people's manners are necessarily better. In other words one should address oneself to the problems that arise, in the company they arise in, without conscious preconceptions and with the object only of finding practicable and generally acceptable solutions.

[1] *Propos de Georges Sorel, recueillis par Jean Variot* (1935), p. 34.

CHAPTER XII

The Civil Service and the Crown

Almost wherever one goes in Europe one sees the tensions and instabilities of the political régime reflected in the administration. If Whitehall seems to have relatively some advantages, it is certainly not because British administrators exhibit any superiority of intelligence or personal integrity, nor of efficiency in the detail of their work. The advantages are not attributable to the administration as such but to the genius of the constitution and to our relatively happy fortunes in war and peace. An administration, considered by itself, is nothing much. Whatever airs it may be tempted to give itself, it is a bit of machinery of which the only worth is in its subordination. If our administration deserves to be tolerated, it is only as it keeps itself near full stretch by its responsiveness, through Ministers, to Parliament, and as it carries out its manifold tasks as part of the implicit unity under the Crown.

The singularity of British government, in these days, rests as much in the conception of the Crown as in the conception of Parliament. The Mother of Parliaments basks in her reputation as a progenitor and model, and because democracy is what people now generally talk of, when they talk of government, no one seeks to deny her a certain importance. It is otherwise with the Crown. The monarch enjoys a world-wide publicity, but no one claims to copy us in the matter of the monarchy. Many pity us, and some of us even pity ourselves, for having retained this merely residual thing. For so the monarchy is generally regarded. Yet no student of government, or even of public administration, can afford to pass lightly over the notion of the Crown, nor to take it too readily for granted that the smooth-worn phrase, that Civil Servants are servants of the

The Civil Service and the Crown

Crown, has no meaning that has any practical significance. We have a traditional monarchy, and we have a Civil Service of a certain kind. There might be connections, to put the thing no higher.

In one sense it may be said that countries which have not retained the monarchy have had to invent something of the same kind, and that Civil Servants everywhere are the instruments of an executive which looks upwards to a head of the state. The intendants of the French monarchy become the prefects of Napoleon and the prefects of the later Republics. We talk of democracy when we talk of government, because that is the most widely acceptable part of it and a wide public is always listening, but elections and popular assemblies are, quantitatively if not qualitatively, among the less important parts of government in a modern industrial state. Maine, it will be remembered, spoke of democracy as 'inverted monarchy'.[1] The main work of government is done by an executive, and where the work is of any complexity that executive must include a large and permanent body of officials. The triumph of democracy in Britain, if it has had a triumph here, is not to have got the work of government done by any popularly elected body but to have informed a large permanent executive with responsiveness to the moods of the elected and of the electorate. Our large bureaucracy is a constitutional nonentity precisely in order that it can serve in this way. A suspicion that it is none the less not absolutely nothing remains. And indeed it is something. But its positive qualities rob nothing from the function of the popular element in government.

The positive qualities of the Civil Service are in general little understood, whether in Whitehall itself or by students. It is customary for both friends and critics of the service to exaggerate the initiatives that are possible in certain directions and to attribute to Civil Servants the wrong sort of responsibility. Of course the administrator knows a subject, or rather, he gets to know in turn a number of subjects, in the sense that, in a certain field or in certain fields, he knows better than anyone how the game has to be played out, between the pressures of various interests, the law, and the temper of the parties. He

[1] Sir Henry Sumner Maine, *Popular Government* (fifth edition, 1909), p. 59.

151

may allow himself a measure of enthusiasm for what is, in concrete terms, being done, particularly if he can persuade himself that what he is doing represents some kind of non-controversial good, as may be the case in the administration of some of the social services. The admirer of the administration may think of the administrator as a man who plays a useful and positive rôle in this social service. The critic will ask rudely who this fellow is who forces ideas upon the public, on his Minister, and on Parliament, because they happen to be to his own personal taste. The critic is nearer to understanding the proper processes of administration than is the enthusiastic admirer. Certainly there are administrators in love with the doings of their own Departments, or of some bit of their Departments, and a little flirtation of this kind may keep the administrator from dying unnoticed where he sits and will certainly render his work more tolerable to him. But this sort of flirtation should on no account be allowed to become a *grande passion*. The administrator who loves his schemes is a nuisance. He will press them on Ministers in season and out of season, using all the professional skills which are meant to facilitate objectivity in such a way as to conceal from those he advises the subjectivity of his approach. The most serious responsibility of the administrator is to lay aside his preferences in favour of an objective assessment of the situation, not in terms of anything he may hold to be good but in terms of the game as it is played in Whitehall. This game, which sometimes looks so obscure in its detail, is the only notion of the good he has right to.

In a particular operation, the end-game often appears to the administrator as a parliamentary one. There are, however, kinds of work where the perspective looks different, either because the subject-matter of it is of little interest to Parliament or because it is something on which the two sides of the House are so much in agreement that prospective disagreements in that quarter do not look very large to the man who is doing the business. For a man who is trying to make a trade agreement, or doing certain sorts of work in relation to foreign affairs or finance, there may be certain parliamentary points to watch but, on the whole, his attention will be fixed on the foreign competitor, on the potential enemy, or on mere figures. The game for him may be the classic game of Richelieu or Machiavelli, though played in the context so different from theirs. It is the game in which the basic assumption is the existence of the realm as a separate entity, and the official is bent above all on keeping it afloat among its neighbours. This, however, is the ultimate assumption too of the administrator whose work is more closely tied to parliamentary affairs. The parliamentary end-game is not an end-game after all, but is important only because it is the index of forces on whose balance the coherence of the realm depends. The administrator, whatever his immediate task, is playing for the survival of the realm. He may not love the several subject-matters of his successive jobs, but he may without offence love his country, though he had better not think too much even about that, lest he put a merely personal construction on the rôle he has to play. He had best think merely of his work, and of the Whitehall game. His devotion to anything more remote had best, in general, be implicit rather than explicit.

The clarity with which the administrator can be seen in the rôle of a servant of the national entity depends no doubt on the job he is doing. Certainly not all Civil Service administrators look like that, all the time; certainly they should not try to. What we have called a 'rôle' is rather a characterization of the basic assumptions of the Civil Servant's job. It is not a matter of the emotions. No doubt the Civil Servant had better not have more of the emotions of loyalty than he can help. They might be more of a nuisance in him than in anyone. The assumptions we speak of are not of the emotions. They are in the logic of his position. He is paid to do what is in effect a technical job of some importance in the business of keeping the state together, of ensuring the continuance of this country as an entity. There are awkwardnesses if one presses home the classifications too far, but it is generally true that this rôle is the distinguishing mark of the Civil Service administrator. The rôle is to be identified by the width of the context in which the Civil Servant works. The context in which, say, the academic student of public affairs works is at once wider and more personal; that in which the man of industrial or commercial affairs works may be narrower and, in a less profound sense, individual. In a large industrial concern the individuality may tend to disappear, and the context may be wide enough to take account of a national interest. But even in a nationalized undertaking the mere survival of the state will not be—and should not be—at the centre of the administrative terms of reference as it is, properly, at the centre of those of the Civil Servant. It is arguable that this consideration, indispensable though it is, may in its manifestations be timorous and negative, and may appear as a fear of breaking something rather than as a passion to secure the survival of something greater. For this reason devices to secure a measure of national surveillance without detailed Civil Service control have an importance of their own. From this point of view the work of the Swedish agencies, and certain decentralizing tendencies elsewhere, may have a value left out of account in the present study, which is concerned with administration as seen from the point of view of central government.

It might well be thought a frivolity to inquire whether this legitimate concern with the continuance of the realm, which characterizes the work of the administrator in the Civil Service and gives him his genuine indifference to party, is more than accidentally connected with the fact that he is what is called a servant of the Crown. Does the Crown mean anything at all in this context? There is a marked disinclination, which did not begin in our days, to regard it as anything more than a show. Bagehot was of this mind. In his language, the Queen was dignified; that meant she was for fools to goggle at. As there were a lot of fools, that counted for something. Indeed Bagehot seems to have estimated the number of those who were not fools as being, in his day, not more than ten thousand.[1] These read *The Economist* and formed a freemasonry of republicans. Bagehot has had a prolonged success, so that one might be tempted to think that the constitution, so sensitive to everything that is said about it, has adapted itself to his views. At any rate we find Ivor Jennings, who is by way of being an authority on the Constitution and who represents what reasonable people think about it nowadays, saying without turning a hair that 'the existence or absence of a monarch does not in itself make a fundamental difference in a Constitution'.[2] This

[1] Walter Bagehot, *The English Constitution* (The World's Classics, 1936), p. 6.
[2] Ivor Jennings, *Cabinet Government* (second edition, 1951), p. 303.

The Civil Service and the Crown

sounds true, in the sense that it is the kind of remark you could make in polite society without startling anybody; it rests, however, more on acceptable opinion, on the temper of the age, than on demonstrable facts, and indeed covers a reality of great complexity. There is nothing intrinsically absurd about holding a different opinion. Bagehot had it that it is a 'fiction that ministers are, in any political sense the Queen's servants'.[1] Jennings can even say: 'The functions of the head of the state, be he King or president, are ancillary.'[2] From a certain point of view, yes. But that point of view is no less arbitrarily chosen than is Clarendon's, when he says: 'Kings having still all that power remaining in them, that they have not themselves parted with, and released to their subjects, and their subjects having pretence to more liberty or power than the King hath granted and given them.'[3] That also rests upon an opinion, though of a kind less familiar in our day. The reality is perhaps best seized by entertaining both opinions and then dropping them both. For our purposes what is important is the possibility of demonstrating that there is a functional relationship between the Queen and the officials of the Civil Service which would make the assertion that the latter are Crown servants no more unmeaningful than declarations of subordination usually are.

The Queen, it is said or used to be said, rules through her Ministers, and it is a perfectly intelligible proposition that she does not rule any the less for that, just as Ministers are not the less Ministers because they exercise their functions in the main through officials. But the Queen, it will be said, does not attend to the details of her country's administration. The Minister does not attend to the details of his Department's administration. It would be a true anachronism for him to do so. It would be a true anachronism for the Queen to express her preferences in the million and one topics that come before her government.

---

[1] Bagehot, p. 11.
[2] Jennings, p. 803.
[3] Clarendon, *A Brief Story of the Leviathan*, p. 89. Cf. 'prerogative, however circumscribed by convention, must always retain its historic character as a residue of discretionary authority to be employed for the common good.' (D. Lindsay Keir, *The Constitutional History of Modern Britain, 1485–1937*, third edition, 1946, p. 491).

She has one inalienable function, which is to secure the coherence of her country. The Minister performs his function more by taking advice and bowing before facts than he does by giving advice and making facts bow before him. And so with the Queen though she, certainly, is so exactly at the centre of the national system of pressures that she has, ordinarily, much less room for movement than a Minister. Her quiescence is the very principle of order. In the course of her duty of securing the coherence and continuity of her realm, the controversies which overturn parties are of no account. 'The Queen's service must be carried on', now this way, now that, to please the whim of party and populace, but that is only because, if those whims are not appeased, there will be disorder and the service will be broken or at an end. The Queen's duty perhaps demands any submission except what will break the realm.

In this scheme of things, the reins of authority meet in the Queen's hand. All the other authorities are subordinate and derivative from her. If the Commons unseat a government, she takes other advisers because her duty is to govern in a manner that will be tolerated. Jennings makes much of what he calls a new principle. He says that a fundamental change came with the Reform Act. Before it, the government reposed in the Sovereign's confidence; afterwards, on the people's. There are historical refinements, evidently, in the position before the Reform Bills and after. But there never was a time when a government had not to be tolerable if it was to endure. James II's popery made his power crumble under his feet. It is not the Reform Bills themselves, but the urbanization and literacy which produced them, which made it necessary latterly for the monarch to listen as attentively to the murmurings of the people as formerly to the growls of the nobility. It is the notorious complexity of a modern administration which has caused the monarch to 'release to his subjects' (in Clarendon's phrase) so many powers.

The maxim that the Queen's service must be carried on means, among other things, that it is of greatly more importance that there should be a government in Britain than that its complexion should be that of one or another party. It is of the nature of party politics to exaggerate and exacerbate differences and to represent policies, which are merely an aspect of things, as the thing itself. The thing itself is the great *res publica* whose continuance the Queen wills. She wills, all the time, all those laws which, by and with the advice of the Lords Spiritual and Temporal, and the Commons, she or her predecessors have enacted and have not repealed. She wills the continuance of all those rights she has protected without enactment. While she broods over this body of laws and institutions, and her servants daily perform the acts which constitute the life and continuance of that corpus, the party managers come along with their medicines and their scalpels to purge or trim some corner of it. The activity of the most fevered session of the House amounts to no more than that. Much is made of these adjustments, and much ought to be made; but more ought always to be made of the great work of time which is the subject of these meddlesome but necessary treatments.

It is recognized by Bagehot and Jennings that recent times are (to put it no higher) not marked by any weakening of the executive's powers. Bagehot and Jennings, however, have in effect chosen to place the head of the executive at an intermediate point in the chain of command. They have said virtually that the cabinet is the beginning and end of government. They have done this partly, no doubt, out of a horror they feel for the supreme, though not for the penultimate heights. Partly, however, they are motivated by an inability to admit a principle of government to which the most exalted advices on our day-to-day affairs would be subordinate. They both have the publicist's touch, and for the publicist day-to-day affairs have a final dignity. Moreover, these matters are those which the popular will, whether of ten thousand or ten million, is supposed mainly to busy itself about and by which it is mainly evidenced. And the cabinet, even if at a couple of removes, reflects what the people are supposed to think about these matters.

But if the recognition of the importance of the executive means anything at all, it means that the fact that the cabinet reflects in some measure a popular will of some sort is the least characteristic thing about it. The cabinet is a government not because it is an outcome of certain electoral procedures but because it governs. What a government loses when it ceases to be regulated or modified by an electoral procedure is not the power to govern but a certain advisory force which tells it what the people will stand. It can go on governing but henceforth it has to rely exclusively on other means of informing itself when the worm will turn. Whatever politicians may make out of the electoral procedures which may result in their losing their jobs, an electorate which votes in such a way that an existing cabinet is overthrown is not saying that it will not continue to be governed substantially according to the same laws as before. It is in effect not objecting to the things that in general are done but in a greater or less measure to the way in which some of them are done. The Crown in short remains; the Constitution remains; the officials, who are ultimately the Queen's servants and not the politicians', raise their eyebrows and continue as before, only noting that certain emphases must be changed.

The constitutional developments of recent times, and still more the spread of literacy and the frequent allusions to acts of government in even the most widely circulated of the papers called newspapers, have obscured the fact that the so-called popular character of our modern governments is an historical accident. Popular institutions are—to use a word which Jennings misapplies to the head of the state—ancillary. It would be perfectly possible to govern England without Parliament or elections though it would certainly not be possible to govern it in this way for long with any efficiency At first there would be merely a prolongation of the administrative peace of the parliamentary recesses. Then, when new legislation was required, it would take the form of Orders in Council. The Departments, carefully consulting the outside world, would produce the material for these enactments as they do for enactments of any kind. Ministers, appointed by the Crown at its own full choice or on the nomination of specially appointed Commissioners, would come to their offices to decide important matters. Briefed by the officials, they would continue to explain things to the press, to their correspondents, and to those who came to see them in deputation. They would meet from time to time in committees, which would be the Cabinet and its com-

The Civil Service and the Crown

mittees. There would be a chief among them, who would be Prime Minister, and they would look through him to the head of the state who would give unity and continuity to their miscellaneous acts. Elections, and an elected House of Commons, do not produce a government. They merely modify it. They inform it with life and even with information and it would be wilful ignorance and, in the strict sense, an imbecility for a government to try to dispense with these resources. None the less, a government conducted without them would be less ill-informed than is commonly imagined about the impact of its proposals. Even at present, with the extra-parliamentary consultations that take place, 'many wills', as Keir rightly says, 'mingle with that of Parliament in the making of a law'.[1]

The general horror with which the pure theory of government has always been regarded—well illustrated by the *succès de scandale* of Machiavelli—is by no means without foundation. It is obscurely felt that to talk too openly of these matters is likely to have an unfortunate effect on the way in which government is in fact conducted, just as it is felt that too public a recognition of our private lusts may end in an intolerable disorder. But just as it is salutary not to deceive ourselves about our sexual appetites it is salutary to remember that, politically, we live in a system of force modified, as the expression of our appetites is modified, by traditions as ancient as our race. Some notion of this sort must lie behind any satisfactory theory of public administration.

The limitations of the tolerance in the state are expressed primarily in the sovereign, who in some sort represents the terms of reference of Parliament. That there should still be a family of England, as there was formerly a family of France, or Spain, or Austria, is odd but not necessarily absurd. That the centre of our terms of reference should be a person and not some theoretical entity or declaration of rights might well commend itself to an age inclined to positivism. It is an arrangement, certainly, which suits the fact-loving temper of the Civil Service.

[1] Keir, p. 463.

159

Index of Names

Index of Names